Susan Hale, Edward Everett Hale

Young Americans Abroad

Being a Family fFlight by Four Young People and their Parents through France and Germany

Susan Hale, Edward Everett Hale

Young Americans Abroad

Being a Family fFlight by Four Young People and their Parents through France and Germany

ISBN/EAN: 9783337211882

Printed in Europe, USA, Canada, Australia, Japan

Cover: Foto ©Andreas Hilbeck / pixelio.de

More available books at **www.hansebooks.com**

YOUNG AMERICANS ABROAD

Being a Family Flight by four young people and their parents through France and Germany

BY
EDWARD EVERETT HALE AND SUSAN HALE

ILLUSTRATED

BOSTON
LOTHROP PUBLISHING COMPANY

CONTENTS.

	PAGE
CHAPTER I. ARE YOU READY? GO!	15
CHAPTER II. ON DECK	24
CHAPTER III. HOW IT CAME ABOUT	31
CHAPTER IV. WHAT CAME ABOUT	41
CHAPTER V. THE VOYAGE	49
CHAPTER VI. THE BELLS	60
CHAPTER VII. THE ARRIVAL	66
CHAPTER VIII. DEAR PARIS	76
CHAPTER IX. SIGHT-SEEING	83
CHAPTER X. A VISIT	96
CHAPTER XI. VERSAILLES	107

Contents.

CHAPTER XII.
Tommy's Lark 116

CHAPTER XIII.
The Louvre 123

CHAPTER XIV.
Last Days in Paris 135

CHAPTER XV.
Out of France 144

CHAPTER XVI.
Into Germany 151

CHAPTER XVII.
Christmas 160

CHAPTER XVIII.
Mr. Hervey 170

CHAPTER XIX.
Weimar 181

CHAPTER XX.
Dresden 192

CHAPTER XXI.
St. Elizabeth 205

CHAPTER XXII.
Eisenach 214

CHAPTER XXIII.
A Bomb 223

CHAPTER XXIV.
Berlin 234

YOUNG AMERICANS ABROAD

CHAPTER I.

ARE YOU READY? GO!

"HERE is Tom!"

It was certainly the fifth time that this question has been asked since breakfast. To the somewhat excited apprehension of Mr. Horner, it seemed the twentieth. For Mr Horner, though a man of affairs, was a little thrown off his balance, now.

"I don't care where he is," said he. "Let him stay with the newsboys, if he wants to."

The occasion was the filing under sheds, between piles of oranges and cotton bales, newsboys and draymen, of a procession, male and female, old and young, which tumbled out, both hands of everybody full, from carriages on the street, and in disorderly order came in sight of the black hull of the *St. Laurent*, on the outside of the landing-sheds of the Compagnie Générale Trans-Atlantique. This procession was the Horner family, leaving New York for Havre. Tom was the youngest of this family, and he had now disappeared for the fifth time since breakfast.

"Never fear for Tom," said Philip, who had risen to the emergencies of a departure, and allied himself to the side of authority. "Never fear for Tom, I will see to him as soon as I leave mamma's things in her state-room. This way, mamma. This way, Bessie. Papa, you are quite wrong."

For Phil had been on board three times already with other boys from

AT THE PIER.

Mr. Newell's school, on one pretext or another, and was proud of being the pilot.

Across the gangway, where even the most timid could not tremble; between chattering French *bonnes* and dirty travelling pedlars; declining endless invitations to purchase rosebuds, neglecting all overtures from

A "ROSEBUD" BOY.

white-aproned waiters, who wished to take from him his mother's umbrella, camp-stool, novel, Bible, and plaid which, at the last moment, Phil had taken in charge, he threaded the way through the large, dark saloon. He pushed between a box of Apollinaris water and a steward with a tray, carrying champagne; he threw open a state-room door, and said with exultation, "There!" This was the large and spacious apartment of which Mrs. Horner had heard so much. Alas for human expectations and the limitations of language!

"Now," said Phil, "I will find Tom."

In Jacob Abbott's travelling directions the instructions for finding a lost boy are these: "Look for him where the monkeys are." These directions Phil remembered. But there were no monkeys within a mile of the pier. Phil thought of the steerage passengers.

He ran down the pier to the place where they were buying their tin mugs, and the rest of their outfit.

For, if you be a child of the public, and travel in the steerage, Europe requires none of the long preparations which luxury exacts. If you are so fortunate as to travel as the masses do, you say at eleven o'clock, "I think I will go across, and see the old folks!" You take an Eight Avenue car up-town, for five cents; you run to the ticket office on the pier, as if it were the ferry to Jersey City, and you buy your ticket there. There is a woman handy at a bench, who will sell you a tin mug, a towel if you need, a basin if you are particular, and a brush and comb if you are luxurious; and having bought these, you go on board. As you cross the gangway, the man in charge cries, "All ashore!" the landsmen leave the ship, and you cross the ocean and see your father. For the Horners, alas! because they were more luxurious, more preparation had been necessary; and so it was that they had lost Tom, and that Phil was in search of him.

But Phil's first dive for Tom was wrong. He was not buying a tin cup nor a wash-basin.

"Here's your nice oranges, seven for a shilling," said a stout woman holding an orange in one hand, and opening a paper box with another.

Phil did not lose his temper, but asked if a little boy had bought oranges. Not a boy had been near the place.

Phil looked for an officer. Nobody but the uniformed men of the steamer were to be seen. They were amused, interested, but stupid; and spoke no language to any purpose, but French.

Phil tried the boys selling newspapers, also, but they were amused, and did their best to sell him. He tried a bootblack with no better luck.

At this moment, a very portly policeman in full metropolitan uniform, strutted with dignity through the spectators and idlers, and touched the gangway man with his baton.

A BOOTBLACK.

"Go and call the ship's doctor!"

The first mate was standing close by, and quickened the man who was underneath: "Vîte, vîte; par ici!" he cried out, pointing to the upper deck, where the doctor was standing. The policeman turned slowly up, saying quietly to the Frenchman. "The boy has broken his leg."

Phil's heart sunk within him. But he rushed up through all the sheds,—jostling porters and expressmen, and steerage people with indifference, — came out into the sunlight, and there was master Tom, sitting on an upturned bucket, with a little dirty baby lying across his knees, whose mother, on her knees, was washing the child's face.

In fact, nobody's leg was broken. That was the policeman's exaggeration. The incident was well-nigh exhausted. Tom had not been able to resist the temptation to help these people out from the furniture wagon which had brought their trunks. The baby was rolled in the mud by a big dog. Tom went into the mud for him, as his costume well indicated. And when Phil led him from the scene in triumph, he was more dirty than he ever remembered to have been before.

"Here's your *Sun,—Herald,—Express,—Graphic*, and all the late second editions, for a quarter!"

"Here's your seven fresh oranges for a shilling!"

"Here's your nice new cups—no soft soder about them—towels, and basins!"

"Please take some flowers," said a shabby girl, courtesying.

But Phil resisted all these syrens.

"Come across the forward passage here, Tom! I can clean you before mamma sees you!"

Actually, the boy succeeded in leading his muddy brother to their state-room undetected. In a minute Tom's valise was open; he was bidden to dress himself in his "next better-most" clothes. Phil loitered on deck, as if unconcerned, just as Mr. Horner was adjusting his wife's arm-chair. Mr. Horner had already forgotten that Tom was lost.

ONE OF THE FLOWER GIRLS.

But Mrs. Horner said, "Oh, Phil, are you there? I was afraid you were lost too. What have you done with Tom?"

"Oh, Tom is in our state-room, mamma. He will be up in a minute."

Thus did the prudent lad save his brother from one reprimand.

"That's better than could be hoped," said his mother. "When they asked for the doctor, I was afraid Tom's neck was broken."

One worry had driven out another, and the boys found, not for the first time, that Tom's absence had not been so much noticed as it really deserved; the cause of **anxiety now was the non-appearance of** Miss Augusta Lejeune.

"I knew it would be so," plaintively said Mrs. Horner. "My plan was a great deal better, that she should spend the night with us and be all ready to start in the morning. To be sure, she hates an early breakfast."

"I never could find out," said Mr. Horner, "why we had it an hour earlier than usual, as the boat does not start till twelve."

"My dear, we should never have got here, if we had had a minute less time," rejoined his wife.

He looked at his watch. "It is only half-past eleven," he said. "She is sure to be here."

They were all anxious, though. The two girls, Mary and Bessie, stood watching the streams of people passing up the gangway, hoping to catch a glimpse of Miss Lejeune, while they kept up a desultory talk with their cousins, who had come to see them off, and who stood about without much to say, beyond envying them the trip, and urging them to be sure to write. The moment is too confused for deep thought or the interchange of serious sentiment, and it is hard to fill up the time with frivolities.

At last there seemed an unusual movement at the passage way nearest them; the buzz of voices, laughter, and gay chattering; and Miss Lejeune appeared below, escorted by two or three gentlemen and one or two ladies, all carrying bouquets or parcels.

"Here we are," called Philip, leaning over the rail. Miss Augusta looked up and nodded, and with her escort joined them above in a few moments.

"Well, Augusta, I knew you would be late!" reproachfully said Mrs. Horner.

"My dear, there is half an hour yet, but I did mean to be here sooner. It is so hard to get away, though! And we had a lovely breakfast. See all these flowers! What shall I do with them? Mr. Strain, do not hold them any longer. Put them down anywhere.

TRINITY CHURCH.

Has anybody seen my ship-chair? Oh, thank you, Mr. Horner; how thoughtful! Here it is, close by the others. Are we all here? Where is my friend Tommy?"

At this precise moment Tommy appeared from below. A vague thought passed through his mother's mind that those were not the clothes she had seen him in last; but the idea was diverted by talk and introductions, and last words to all the friends.

Mr. Agry, the partner of her father, had a great deal of teasing with Bessie, by way of farewell.

"Now, Bessie, what do you expect to see abroad that will repay you for going?" he asked.

"Oh, a great many things," said Bessie, rather embarrassed.

"Such as what? Come, now," he persisted.

"Well, mountains and churches —" the child began vaguely.

"Churches! now I will venture to bet with you, Bessie, a pound of the best sugar-plums you can buy in Europe that you do not see a single church finer than Trinity church, in New York."

"I do not believe I know how Trinity church looks," replied the frank Bessie, blushing. "I must have passed it ever so many times, but I do not look at these things much."

The laugh was against her.

"Take care and buy yourself a new kind of spectacles," said Mr. Agry, "or when you come back you will not know whether you have gained your bet or not."

Bessie promised to look particularly at churches in all the cities she should visit, and it was agreed that the first thing on her return, Mr. Agry was to take her to thoroughly inspect Trinity church, and pronounce upon its architectural merits, compared with the cathedrals of the old world.

CHAPTER II.

ON DECK.

AND now they could begin to see what wisdom and what folly combines, in a space not large, as three hundred people from one continent leave it for another.

Pretty Miss Wither reclined in her chaise-longue, and received the homage of her admirers, who came to say good-by, while tired Mrs. Wither, her mother, sat bolt upright beside her, and received very little homage. One young gentleman had brought a splendid nosegay, of fifty jaqueminot roses. Another, more modest, had brought fifty white lamarques. Miss Wither, gracious to both, had one in one hand and one in another. Then blushing Mr. Jourdan, more demonstrative, brought fifty moss-roses, and Miss Wither, still trying to be equal in her courtesy, was fain to lay the jaqueminots in her lap, that she might have a hand free for the moss-roses. Young Mr. Macullar sauntered round the group, quite indifferent. But the others all looked as if they would eat him, because he was going on the ship, and would be perpetually in Miss Wither's presence, while, alas! their nosegays would certainly fade. And fade they did; but one, she had promised to keep, lasted longer than the rest.

On the other side the deck was more tragedy. There, sweet, pale Mrs. Lampe, in her widow's cap, was kissing, — she could not kiss often enough, — Agatha and Laura, who were on their way to Wiesbaden to see the grandfather and grandmother whose dear faces they knew so well, but whom they had never seen.

"There's the boy! there's the boy!" cried Mr. Macullar. "This way, this way, quick!"

The boy was bringing Mr. Macullar's hat-box, which had been forgotten at the Windsor.

"Has any one seen a man or a boy from the druggist's at the corner of Twenty-Sixth street?"

This question was drawled out to Phil by an old lady, who, at the last, had telephoned for toilet-powder.

His brother Tom joined him, after his rapid toilet, and, dashed a

HER FAVORITE ROSE.

little by Phil's brief but solid exhortations, which, to say truth, affected the boy more than his father's or mother's did, he kept quite closely glued to him through the half hour which remained to them of America.

Of a sudden the horses on the pier were checked and drawn back, and eight or ten policemen, in a column of two, pressed forward. Two of these men took possession of one gangway, two of another. They would let no one pass either way. Even the orange-men and newsboys, impressed by the spectacle, stopped their clamor and gathered around the gangway, to look on. The commander of the policemen spoke to the mate of the ship, and in a moment more, four of them, with as many men wearing the ship's uniform, were hurried on board.

ORANGE WOMAN.

Phil and Tom were highly excited, and ran and called their father.

"Clearly," he said to them, "they hope to find some fugitive from justice, or some man or woman who is trying to escape to Europe; probably some thief who has stolen valuable property." And as the boys looked on and wondered, they saw, in a minute more, that no one below was permitted to come up to them; that no one on their deck was permitted to go down; no person aft was permitted to go forward, and no person forward, to come aft. In a minute more the captain of the policemen, who wore a newer cap and more gold lace than the others, passed the guard at the companion way and came upon their deck. He touched his hat civilly, two or three times, as he passed gentlemen whom perhaps he knew; he looked very carefully at every one, not coming near to anybody. Then he strode by the boys upon the bridge, and looked down on the forward deck. Alas! in a moment all was over. From the depths of the ship up came a gabbling French sailor in his red shirt sleeves; and behind him followed the poor prisoner, with a parcel done up in a newspaper containing his possessions, and the policeman who had arrested him following the two.

"That is the man," said the officer hastily. "I am much obliged to you, captain."

Then he called to his men below, "Take him to the station! Good-day, sir; good-day, sir," and things began as before.

"Here's your seven oranges for thirteen cents!"

"Here's your *Sun* and *Herald!*" and the boys were left to wonder what had been stolen and what the prisoner's name was. Nobody knew, and, excepting themselves, nobody cared.

And now, very soon, people who were particularly afraid of being carried to France without their own consent, took leave. Miss Lejeune's friends bowed and shook hands; there was much kissing of the two ladies who had accompanied her, and a few last words in a low tone.

"You know, if the lace is eight inches wide it will do. I had rather have the pattern just right, than the width. Still, nine inches is better, you know."

"I know, my dear, exactly what you want; and then I am to give it to the Smiths if they are coming over; and if they spend the winter I shall easily find some one else."

There were plenty of well-wishers for each of the party. Phil's friends and Tom's were, alas! ignominiously caged in their respective schools, where the masters, tyrants that they were, could not be made to say that the sailing of the *St. Laurent* was an occasion of sufficient national importance to justify a holiday. But many of the girl friends of Mary and Bessie were there. And one by one they took Phil aside, and pressed on him little notes for Bessie which he was to keep secret, one till the fourth day, one till the fifth, and one till the sixth of the passage, when they were to be put on her plate at breakfast as a surprise. And, lest Phil should forget, Tom received presents of barley sugar and candied fruit, in return for which he gladly promised to remind Phil. But Phil said, rather grimly and quizzically, that he thought he should remember better than Tom.

Thus there was much chaffing and laughing, but Miss Lejeune, even, was beginning to get tired of it, and Mr. Horner, who was unusually nervous on this occasion, and rather fussy, was bored by all these admirers. He heartily wished they would carry themselves off.

AT THE GUN.

"There is a bell!" he said pointedly, and true enough, something did sound somewhere. Every one started, and the parting-guest-speeders gathered themselves together with renewed hand-shaking and kissing, and promises to write. If the Horners had written all the letters they then agreed to, they would have had no time, through the year of their absence, to go anywhere, or see anything.

The friends now disposed themselves in favorable positions on the pier, for waving of handkerchiefs and other solemnities of good-bye. More hardy people, who had done the same thing often before, waited with audacity, till they should be ordered on shore by the officers. The sailors were at their posts. Few carriages came down the pier, and it was fairly still. For every cabin passenger had come half an hour early, and the steerage people came by street cars, and walked down the pier. But a messenger would hurry up with flowers, or an expressman with state-room stores which had been delayed. And at last, with great fuss and display, came the gaily painted wagon with Uncle Sam's mails. These were bundled on board with much more parade, Phil thought, than the occasion justified. When they were fairly hidden away, Mr. Agry seemed to think the time had come.

"Give yourself no anxiety, old fellow," he said to Mr. Horner, as he gave his hand the last shake; "it will be all right."

"Good-bye, Mrs. Horner," as he turned to her. "If your husband writes a line about business, put it into the fire; if he says a word about it, kill him."

"One kiss, Miss Mary," to that young lady; "you are looking better already."

"Don't forget a yellow feather for your bonnet, Bessie. Rue Tom Dick and Harry, Numéro 99, remember." This was some further nonsense between them.

"My dear Miss Lejeune, why did not you ask me to come? I would have exploded dynamite under the offices, killed all the clients and customers, and joined you gladly.

"Phil, my lad, good-bye; you are the only level-headed person in this crowd. Do not let them work too hard, and take Tom to the Zoo.

"Tom, I heard you were lost, but you seem to be all right. Good-bye, all! Good-bye!"

"All ashore! all ashore!" cried the officer in good French-American dialect.

Mr. Agry ran ashore. The gangway rolled on shore. The bell rang, the whistle sounded and the screw turned slowly. Phil saw, with a certain reverence, the great piston slowly rise. In a moment he and Tom were on the bridge, and the others resting on the rail. Their handkerchiefs were flying, the school-girls on the pier were waving theirs. They could see Mr. Agry tie his upon a stick.

"Are you sick, yet?" cried Emma Fortinbras to Mary, as she waved her parasol. Everybody laughed at Emma's joke, and these were, as it happened, the last words which America addressed to the voyagers.

Phil staid on the bridge till the last handkerchief was out of sight;

30   A FAMILY FLIGHT.

to his surprise and disgust, as he put his own away, he found he was wiping fresh tears from his cheeks. How they came there he did not know. He led Tom to see the man at the wheel.

And so in less than half an hour, the pier was deserted.

A few people to whom the parting was a serious one, since those who now left them were going for a long time, perhaps never to return, lingered at the edge of the water to follow the receding steamer, as, after turning her huge bulk with difficulty, she was under way, and moved off with dignity through the heaving waves. When the long line of smoke was utterly confounded with the masts and confused lines of distance, even these with a sigh turned away, and slowly walked back through the empty warehouses to busy Broadway.

BUSY BROADWAY.

CHAPTER III.

HOW IT CAME ABOUT.

MARY was not very well in the spring. They took her out of school for a while, but she missed the society of the girls, and went back again. Her eyes troubled her when she was over a German dictionary, but she did not think of it when she was reading the novels which would get into the house, although Mrs. Horner did not altogether approve of any of them, and especially not of the fine print of cheap editions.

Decidedly Mary read too much and played too little. She was growing fast, and felt a little superior to the sports of the children, while she found herself shy and silent in the society of older people. She took no interest in breakfast, was apt to be late in the morning, and after looking with scorn upon the cold toast and warmed-over chop, to hastily drink some milk, snatch an apple for luncheon and start off for school, in a state of mind described as "cross" by the younger children. Her mother, having compassion on her, did not call such hard names, but thought this would never do, turned it over and over in her mind, and consulted her friends.

"Why don't you send her abroad," said a chance visitor.

"Don't you think it would be well to send her abroad?" said an elderly friend of the family.

"Change of scene," pronounced the family doctor. "Send her abroad."

In fact a chorus of voices filled the air, echoing, reverberating the advice "send her abroad."

Now this is a very dangerous influence to creep into a family. It soon pervaded the atmosphere, and undermined the stability of the very foundations of the house. There began to be a feeling that perhaps Mary would go abroad, which unsettled the routine of every day. After such an idea was admitted, anything might happen. The very suggestion had given a little extra importance to the girl. She carried her head a little higher, and the color, too rare of late, showed itself in her cheeks. Almost without discussion it came to be an established fact that Mary was to go abroad, but the how, when and where, were still a mighty problem to be solved.

There was in the circle of the family a certain person much valued and considered by them all, young and old. She was not a relative, although called aunt Gus by the younger children, Augusta by the parents. She was supposed to have been an intimate friend of mamma's, ages ago, in that mystical period when she was a girl. Papa seems to have taken kindly to her at the time of his marriage to mamma, and since then she gradually became built into the family. She did not live with them, but in another part of New York, very independently, in rooms by herself. For aunt Gus was not married, but a spinster; one of that valuable class whose merits are growing more and more to be appreciated as the world grows older, and they grow younger; since it is a singular fact that whereas such persons used to be called "old maids" they are now acknowledged to possess the advantage of perennial youth.

Miss Augusta was highly accomplished, well-informed and agreeable. She had been abroad several times, and spoke several languages, "well enough to get along," as she herself expressed it. The very first thing Mrs. Horner thought of about Mary's going, she confessed to her husband, would be to have Augusta take her.

But would Augusta go again and leave her cosy little apartment, all her charities and philanthropies, her book-clubs and cook-clubs, her Decorative and Useful Arts, her tiles and her embroideries? For Miss Lejeune dabbled a little in everything.

Miss Augusta would go. She would sell her shares in the Arizona-Smelting and Mining Company, and go with that. It was now five years since she had tasted Europe, and she would like to try it again, and besides she felt it a duty to relieve poor dear Jeannie

MARY HORNER.

of her worry about Mary. Jeannie was Mrs. Horner. Persuade any single woman that a pleasure is a duty, and she is secured for it.

And now about the heads of the Horners, came tumbling avalanches of advice, suggestion and warning. Guide-books and maps poured in, as it were, at the doors and windows. Experienced travellers talked to them by the hour of what Mary must and must not do, as if the future of the American nation depended upon the arrangement of her plan of travel. Long before they had really begun to think what she should do, or where she should go, or how long she should stay, all these things had been discussed and decided by friends and relatives, far and near, who thus had themselves all the pleasure, and none of the anxieties, of planning the trip.

Mr. Horner contemplated these ominous symptoms rather gloomily, although he had assented at first to the plan. He was very fond of Mary, and liked to have her about. He had never been abroad, and had an idea, perhaps exaggerated, of the size, and especially of the depth, of the Atlantic ocean. On general principles, he disapproved of American girls travelling, and he professed a vague fear that Mary might be snapped up by some foreigner, — by which he meant matrimonially.

But who can resist the attraction of travel, when it once is in the air! Miss Lejeune came round in the evenings, and different routes were discussed. Little time-tables of steamers were lying about, and the conversation turned frequently on the respective merits of the different lines. Mr. Horner was all for a Cunarder. He had always heard they were so safe, and a number of wise saws of the same description, as that Britannia rules the seas; that the English steamers are the best in the world; that the captains sit up all night and change the watch themselves, and that speed is not so important as a steady keel. He was even a little disposed to have them go to Boston and sail from there; since the Boston Cunard steamers, being smaller and dirtier than the New York ones, would be in proportion safer.

Miss Augusta Lejeune, on the other hand, was in favor of the

White Star line. She had been put off with Cunarders, — yes, once even with a Boston Cunarder, — all her life, on account of the safety, and had always longed for a White Star. The reputation of this line is more established every year, and really it was ridiculous in her estimation, to doubt its safety, and to allow such doubts to outweigh the great comfort and enjoyment of the clean, big staterooms, and well-ordered management.

Thus they talked; but as it happened, Miss Augusta even now failed to go by her favorite White Star line. There seemed to be no real reason for going first to England, as one of their settled wishes was to get soon to Paris. The Horners liked to please themselves with the idea that so much outlay and expense was for the benefit of Mary's languages, as well as of her health; it appeared, in one sense, to be a waste of material to be travelling in England, where no dictionary is needed. Miss Lejeune had spent a good deal of time in Paris, and felt more at home there than in London, and then the Stuyvesants were in Paris, old friends, who would be delighted to have Mary come straight to them. And so they one day decided to "cut the little island entirely for the present," as Miss Lejeune expressed it, and to take a state-room in the French steamer *St. Laurent*.

In this way they would avoid crossing the channel, and if they chose to stop at Brest, they would avoid the channel altogether. This was Mr. Horner's proposal, whose feeling was that every drop of the ocean was one drop in the bucket too much; Miss Augusta held her peace, knowing pretty well that when they were fairly on the voyage, twenty-four hours more or less would not make much difference, and that Havre would prove to be, most likely, their destination. Miss Augusta hated so much discussion, though she bore it pretty well. "If only once we get off," she thought a dozen times a day, "we can settle everything as we please."

One thing being established, their steamer, plans began to take a definite aspect; and the delightful task of adopting and rejecting became the sole occupation of the little circle. *Pater familias* was getting interested. He talked Europe with people

MISS AUGUSTA LEJEUNE.

BACHARACH.

down town who convinced him, by turns, of the absolute importance of a great many things. One day he came home full of the Fair at Nidji Novgorod, which they must not miss whatever they did; another time he brought the prospectus of a pension in Bacharach, a small town in the western part of Bavaria, where they could talk the language, and learn more than by any amount of travelling.

On one particular day Mr. Horner came home with an air of something unusual about him. He got through dinner talking less than ordinary, and when towards the end, the children slipped off as they usually did, especially if the pudding lacked attraction, even Mary on this occasion, though she of late stayed to talk with the elders, going away to prepare for a concert,—

"My dear, — " said the father of the family, and then paused.

"Well, what is it, Philip?" said Mrs. Horner. "I see that something is on your mind."

"Well, Jeannie," he continued, then paused again; but added with a jerk, "Brown thinks we had better all go!"

"All go!" repeated Mrs. Horner in amazement.

There was no question in her mind about the words, though they might seem to require amplification. "Go" meant "go abroad" and "all" meant the Horners, *en masse*. The subject had so filled their minds of late that there was no room for any other.

Mrs. Horner gasped a little, and then said calmly, "Why not!"

CHAPTER IV.

WHAT CAME ABOUT.

THUS it was settled that the whole family should go abroad, and this is why they were all to be found on the deck of the steamer *St. Laurent* in the first chapter.

The plan once admitted, excellent reasons were found to cover each member. Mr. Horner needed a change. Stocks had been rising and travelling is always a safe investment. Its dividends are good health and good spirits, funds of information and retrospect, without mentioning photographs and carved work, or the clothes from Paris which are brought back in the trunks of the returning tourists.

BESSIE'S BEST DOLL.

Bessie was delighted. In the original plan, nobody had much thought about her interests. She was one of the plump, easy-going children, whom no one thinks much about, because they have a knack of looking after themselves. She was a year younger than Mary, perfectly well, per fectly good-natured, quiet in her movements, and prone to accept the existing order of things. So she had not grumbled at "all the fuss," as she might have called it, about Mary's health and Mary's trip; but now it was decided that all were to go, her round face beamed like a full moon; she immediately set about packing a small box with her favorite dolls,—for she was one of the girls who kept up her affection for dolls, even to the age of thirteen, and promised herself that pleasure until she should be married.

The oldest son of the family was named Philip, but as this was his father's name, he had come to be called Jack, very generally, no one knew why, exactly. He at once recognized the advantages of a long holiday, and total freedom from school. More than any of the rest, he dwelt on the pleasures of the voyage, and looked forward with impatience to the trip on the steamer. His mother had to caution him, in private, not to talk too much about this part of it before his father, who detested the sea and boats of every description, who visibly flinched whenever he thought of ten days on the steamer, and wished they could wait till balloons, or a tunnel, were invented for crossing the Atlantic.

Master Tommy rejoiced in the general excitement, and that something was going to happen. Mary told him he would have to learn French, or he might starve if he got left by himself anywhere by accident; he therefore applied himself to acquiring the French names for things to eat, but his slight lisp, and heedless ear, prevented any very rapid progress in the language.

It was feared that Miss Augusta Lejeune might not altogether like the change of plan; but she did.

"To tell the truth, Jean, it is a great relief," she said to her friend, as soon as they had a chance to talk it over.

"After the first glow of assenting to go with Mary, I have been torn with anxiety!"

"You worry!" exclaimed Mrs. Horner, "what nonsense; as if single women ever had any real worry."

"I mean on account of the responsibility," continued Miss Lejeune, "if Mary had been homesick, or ill, or anything. Now, you can take care of her, and besides she will not be; and if any admirers make up to her, you can take care of them."

Mrs. Horner laughed: "No, I think I shall leave that department to you. You will know best how to handle them."

"Ah, my dear," replied Augusta, "that is what I want to say now. As you are all going, I think I may as well stay at home. I was the what-do-you-call-it, round which we built the arch, but now it is done, you may as well take me out."

She said this lightly and pleasantly, but before her sentence was half through, Mrs. Horner began to interrupt her, hastening to say:

"What nonsense, Augusta, we were afraid you might begin to talk like that; but we shall not hear of it. Philip says he should not think of going without you, and I'm sure I shouldn't. We have neither of us been abroad, and we depend upon you entirely, and as for the children — "

More was said of this sort, and it may be that Miss Lejeune only felt the need of being urged a little; for she soon gave in, only ending the subject by saying as she laughed, "Very well, then, I go in the capacity of female courier to the party."

After this all was bustle and joy for the children, and bustle and misery for the parents. The servants all gave warning at once, though the greatest pains had been taken to shut the door whenever the subject was to be discussed; but Tommy admitted telling his nurse that he was going to Africa, he believed, one Saturday night when she was emptying his pockets.

The house, which was advertised to be let, was overrun by applicants coming to look at it, whose only real object seemed to be finding out what was kept in the closets. When it was let, which luckily happened at once, it had to be put all in apple-pie order, and every housekeeper knows what that means. Mrs. Horner was quite worn out.

But the worst of all was the advice of friends, which had indeed begun very early in the matter, and the quantity of comforts for the voyage which poured in upon this travelling family. Mary received four brush-bags, three shoe-bags, seven catch-alls, and nine omnium-gatherums, all to be nailed on the walls of her state-room. The other members of the family got almost as many, and while they were trying to persuade themselves that they would all be useful, Miss Lejeune roundly ordered that every one must be left at home, as superfluous on the voyage, and a perfect nuisance after you got anywhere.

POOR MAMMA.

Some of the things people gave them however were good. An india-rubber bottle with a screw-top, to hold hot water for the feet, Miss Augusta said one day might go, "although," she added " I never need any of these things, but you may some of you be sick."

Mr. Horner left the room, as he always did when the voyage was mentioned. The others laughed, and Mary said, " poor papa! I feel as if I were dragging him to the stake."

" Never you mind," cried Miss Lejeune, " he will like the stake well enough when he gets to it; I dare say it will be still harder to bring him home again!"

The fact is that for the Atlantic voyage, which after all is but a matter of ten or eleven days, it is unwise to encumber the small staterooms with superfluous things. Take of course everything you want, but why accompany your toilet on these days with machinery which stands untouched on your dressing-table, year in and year out? If a sea-passenger is sick, the very sight of these decorations of the cabin is odious to him, and it is a burden to have to move them about when they are in the way, as they always are, of his tottering steps. If by good luck he is well and jolly, the last thing he desires is to stay one minute longer than necessary in his close and stuffy state-room. The deck is the goal he longs for in the morning when he hears the water splashing and slopping about over his head, as the sailors are scrubbing it down. A brief, though thorough toilette, is all he can stay for, in his haste to reach the bracing breeze above, for a brisk walk of several turns up and down before breakfast.

Thus discoursed Miss Augusta Lejeune, the wary old voyager; but she allowed the excellence of a few things, sea-chairs on the deck, lots of wraps and rugs, a good novel or two, and above all a bottle of smelling salts, the kind called "Preston" being her favorite.

"My dear," she said to any "dear" in general who might chance to be on hand, "you can have no conception of the immense number of bad smells that keep coming. There are periods when every smell seems to be a bad one, and then, if you can just put your salts to your nose for a moment you tide over the sensation, and very likely you are all right again."

Mr. Horner was so much impressed with this that he ordered a gross of smelling-salts of the kind she described, and thus each member of the family was supplied. Miss Augusta herself had an imposing bottle with a gold top, which some one had given her for her first voyage; but she declared that the common ones were much better, as indeed they were.

A flower-pot, containing a tall and branching plant, a sure preventive of sea-sickness, the gift of an anxious admirer of Mrs. Horner, was left at home. A miniature edition of Shakespeare in thirty-seven volumes, was left out of the state-room valise, and it is feared never crossed the water. Bessie petitioned hard for her favorite game of Authors, consisting of fifty cards, and Miss Lejeune reluctantly yielded this point.

"But you will hate them," she groaned, "when the ship is rolling some day, and every one of the fifty cards comes sliding down from the shelf into a different place under the sofa." And this prediction was verified, on the third day out.

On the whole, the packing and preparations went on very well. As soon as the decision was made for a general departure, an early time was fixed for sailing. Luckily the French steamers were running not very full at that time and excellent state-rooms were secured for all **the** party in the *St. Laurent*, sailing October first.

It was not without much discussion, and inspection of different lines, that Mr. Horner made the difficult decision in favor of this one. Where

AN EXCURSION STEAMER.

all are so good, chance is perhaps the best guide in selecting. Miss Lejeune sighed as she thought of her beloved White Stars, but her familiarity with the French steamers, in one of which she "had crossed" before, consoled her.

One of the steamers was at the wharf at the time they were making up their minds, and Jack and Tommy went with their father to inspect it, and see what kind of accommodations there were for the passengers. It was a beautiful day, the harbor was full of ferry-boats and excursion steamers, the sea rough, but sparkling and bright, tempting them to cross the Atlantic at once. The boys gazed with awe at the immense size of the hull, and with wonder at the extreme smallness of the cabins; the two were to share one state-room, and they were a good deal impressed with the limited space to put all their things. Jack, who had a reflective turn, went home, and considerably reduced the pile of indispensables he had set aside to be packed for him. Tommy, who never reflected at all, described joyfully the ladder by which he was to ascend to his upper berth.

The day came. It was fine. The tide served to sail at noon, so they had all the morning before them. Mr. and Mrs. Horner, the girls and Tommy, were packed into the carriage, while Jack mounted with the driver. This was because Mrs. Horner, turning nervous at the last, could not bear to be separated from her family. For the same reason, the luggage, twelve large trunks, and the three portmanteaus for the voyage, followed close on behind in an express wagon. Miss Lejeune was to meet them at the boat (a horrible arrangement, Mrs. Horner thought), but it could not well be otherwise, as she was receiving a parting breakfast from a few of her intimate friends. However she was sure to be there in time.

So they drove off, the neighbors looking out of windows, for it was quite a procession, the servants waving aprons and smiling, the cook shedding a few natural tears. Ann, the nice woman who had been with them for years, came out to the carriage with an armful of wraps, tucked the mamma into her place, poked handbags under the seats, scolded the girls a little, gave a final tug to Tommy's cort, and shut the door with a bang. The impatient horses departed at the sound.

They started off down the street, the family looked back waving and nodding. Ann seemed to be making frantic signs to the driver. Something must be forgotten. With infinite pains he was induced to stop: she screamed out to him:

"Be sure you don't miss the boat."

That was all.

And he did not.

NEIGHBOR AT WINDOW.

CHAPTER V.

THE VOYAGE.

THEY were off. The pier looked in the distance like the smallest speck, and waving handkerchiefs were indiscriminate among masts and smoke. Even the fondest love could descry no further sign of the vanishing friends, and the passengers now turned to see what could be made of their present surroundings for consolation or amusement.

There is a sad element in the departure of a steamer, even when you are accompanied by all your household gods. Mrs. Horner sat with her handkerchief near her eyes. The girls stood quietly by her side. Tommy and Jack were with their father at the stern of the ship, the former leaning over the side to watch the churning of the screw upon the foamy water.

Miss Lejeune was already scanning the deck, to find out, if possible, the nature of their fellow passengers, and the chance of agreeable companions, but not much was to be learned as yet, for only a few were scattered about upon the seats. Almost every one was below, "shaking down" into the cabins; and, to create a diversion, she proposed that they should follow this example. Hand-bags, shawl-straps, bouquets, were now assembled, and an inspection was made of the premises. Nothing could be more convenient than the arrangement of their state-rooms, the girls close to their mother, the boys not far off, Miss Lejeune near at hand.

On the French steamers, the *salle à manger* stretches across the stern of the ship, with windows all round, just under the upper deck. This brings all the state-rooms down below, opening on long narrow passages running the whole length of the vessel. There are no deck state-rooms, but those below are large and comfortable, each with a sofa which may be a third berth.

Mrs. Horner privately thought them very small, and could not imagine why the term "large" had been used in their description. She wondered how she could ever get through ten days in that "mite of a place," but decided she should pass most of the time on deck. Alas! that day was not over before she was glad to come back to her cabin, and it was some days before she made a regular appearance in the dining-room.

But it is not worth while to dwell on the early sufferings of the Horner family during the voyage. Suffice it to say that after three days t h e y were all acclimated, and ready to enjoy the delightful life on the ocean waves. Miss Augusta is never sick; her example, and the salt water plunge bath which it is always possible to have on the French steamers, kept the two girls well up to the mark. Mary, the delicate, was the one who minded least the motion. Bessie — but we are to say nothing of that. As for Mr. Horner, it was wonderful how he enjoyed it. All his dread of the mighty Atlantic vanished. He was the first on

STERN OF STEAM-SHIP.

THE STEAMER

deck in the morning, the gayest of the party at breakfast, and always all day in the best of spirits. Freedom from routine and the cares of business was, most unexpectedly, so great a relief to his mind, that his wife began to think the great merit of the trip was going to be this renewal of his youth and spirits.

One morning, about four days out, our party assembled for the first time in a bevy on deck, in the place where it afterwards became their custom to establish themselves. It was the first appearance of Mrs. Horner. She was carefully installed in her sea-chair, and tucked in with wraps. Now was the time to put to use all the travelling appliances given her by anxious friends. The india-rubber hot water bottle was at her feet; a patent air-cushion at her back, a knit head-rest behind her, a crochet affghan on her knees, an embroidered shawl upon her shoulders; a marvellous sea-hood protected her ears, an uncut French novel was on her lap, and the celebrated Preston salts in her hand.

"Now, mamma," said Mary, "you look like the typical traveller, "and we shall leave you for our usual exercise on deck."

Mary already had a soft color in her cheeks and looked gay and animated. Bessie was waiting for her below, outside the saloon window and the two started off, to make the whole length of the deck to the bows; no slight excursion, and excellent exercise when repeated half-a-dozen times or more.

"That old lady has come out of her state-room, and is sitting in there," said Bessie. "I was going in to write some more on my letter, but she looks so pale and miserable, I guess I will leave her alone."

"Oh yes, come along and walk," said Mary. "You will have plenty of time for your letter."

Mr. Horner settled himself near his wife and Miss Lejeune, who was sitting upright without any wraps or veils, closely buttoned into a thick tightly fitting jacket, with her book at her side and her knitting in her hand. A strip of plain knitting, about four inches wide was the inevitable companion of Miss Lejeune. Yards upon yards fell from her rapid needles. No one knew what became of the stripes. She always said they were for an affghan, but the affghan

was never seen. She now began, in a low voice, to point out some
of their fellow passengers, and to describe them, as far as she could,

BESSIE.

at present. Tommy came and sat down at his mother's feet, and
Phil lingered about to join in the talk.

"Those people are Germans," said Miss Augusta; "odd they should be on a French steamer. I think they are Jews. See the diamonds! That fat one is the mother of the little ones, I think — their noses are so exactly alike, all of them — but I guess the daughters are by another marriage, for they don't treat the mother very well.'

MR. LEVI

"There's the father," said Jack. "He is named Mr. Levi. I heard the steward call him so."

The captain was walking up and down upon the bridge, a stout man, with a gold band round his cap.

"He is real cross," said Tommy. "I fell against his legs once, and asked his pardon, and he did not say it was no consequence."

"Did you try him in French, Tom?" asked his mother.

"See," said Jack, "I think that is a very nice family sitting over on the other side. They are near us at table, and they seem very jolly, now they are over being sick."

It was all very bright and pleasant on deck. The sun was shining, a soft wind was blowing, but it was not too cold with wraps. The gentle thumping of the screw came in like an undertone suggesting steady progress, with the wash of the water along the sides of the ship. The sea was covered with bobbing little waves, and all around, in every direction, nothing was to be seen but the great round world of water, and the bright glowing sky shutting down over it. Sails in the distance, and as yet birds occasionally, were the only objects to be seen, except the plunging porpoises that sometimes followed their course, humping their curved backs out of the water, like a school of submarine boys turning somersaults.

MARY'S FIRST SKETCH.

On the deck of the *St. Laurent* all was tranquil. Little groups of passengers chatted together, enjoying the scene, counting the bells, which strike every half-hour, and either dreading or longing the approach of luncheon time.

THE VOYAGE.

Mary even attempted, in her sketch-book, a few studies of attitudes in charcoal, without much success.

"That reminds me," said Miss Lejeune, "that I have made an acquaintance at dinner, and I want to show him to you. We have had our end of the table quite to ourselves once or twice, and had a good deal of talk. He is Mr. Hervey; don't you remember the Herveys we met at Mount Desert once? They are Boston people,

MT. DESERT.

I seem to remember, and I should think so by his accent; in fact I believe they have the very best Boston grandmothers. Anyhow he is agreeable, and is apparently alone, but perhaps all his party are below."

Pretty soon Mr. Hervey came along, and was introduced all round. He proved to be the very man with whom Mr. Horner had smoked

58   A FAMILY FLIGHT.

the first cigar he ventured upon. They were soon laughing and talking of the miseries and comforts of the voyage, and before it was clearly understood how things got so far, Tommy was perched upon the new gentleman's knee. For Tommy, though he was getting a big boy, retained some of the habits of a baby.

Mr. Hervey proved a valuable addition to their party. He was alone, and confessed he liked travelling alone, and picking up his companions as he went along. Mr. Horner liked him. They shared those mysterious rites of smoking and shaving and discussing stocks which occupy men when they are left to themselves. Mrs. Horner liked him because he was nice with the children, and for

BRUNO'S ESCAPE.

the same reason he was liked by the children themselves. Mary, the reserved and dreamy, and the easy-going Bessie, alike took him into favor. Philip thought he was "splendid," and Tommy must have bored him dreadfully, for there was no moment when he was not close at his heels. But he never betrayed any such feeling, though he had a skilful way of disengaging himself when he chose, by attracting the boy's attention to something far off on the ship. Very early in their acquaintance, he introduced the young people to the live-stock in the forward part of the steamer. There were cocks and hens, turkeys, lambs, and an immense great dog not allowed to move about, but shut up in the charge of the butcher. It is quite surprising how often he reminded Tom of these animals, and fostered the interest which Tom readily got in their welfare. Perhaps the butcher did not enjoy it as well as the others did at their end of the ship. There was some little stir one day when our young friend let the dog loose, in the interests of humanity, and as a member of the S. P. C. A., so that he rushed up on deck and came suddenly in contact with the legs of a second class passenger, who was taking his first walk after sickness, and rather unsteady. It took several sailors, and a good many minutes, to secure Master Bruno, and put him back in his place. Tom prudently retreated from the scene, and never was actually known, though suspected, to be the author of the mischief.

It is well to be able to record that none of the party were very seriously affected by sea-sickness, and that after some days every one was in good condition to enjoy the fine weather and the excellent table of the *St. Laurent*. They readily fell in with the French system which is in use on the steamers of this line.

CHAPTER VI.

THE BELLS.

EVERY morning Michel, the steward, brought a cup of coffee and a crooked Vienna roll to the berth of each of the ladies. Michel was a vivacious, lean little Frenchman, clad in dark blue, with alert and softly gliding steps, who fulfilled the duties of a chambermaid very adroitly, making the beds, tucking in and turning down the blankets, with more than the skill of a woman.

In France, the Horners got used to seeing this, but at first this man-maid was an anomaly. Michel was very obliging, and it was cheering to have him come in every morning, with his *plateau* and "bon jour!"

A good comfortable breakfast at nine or later, and dinner at four, were the meals of the day. There was lunch at some time between, but the Horners, except Tommy, seldom went down to it, preferring to pass the long day on deck, and here after dinner they again assembled, having the coffee brought to them then. And this was the pleasantest part of the whole, comfortably digesting a good dinner, reposing on well arranged chairs and pillows, with plenty of wraps, to see the day pale and the stars come out, chatting gayly or quietly on all possible subjects. Every one was surprised to find how agreeable every one else was; there was plenty of time to talk and think, and discuss, which is seldom the case in our busy American life.

At four bells in the evening the little party broke up, for only Tommy was sent off earlier. Mrs. Horner and the girls went to bed at once and slept like tops. Mr. Horner smoked a final cigar, at this time, while Miss Lejeune and Mr. Hervey had a way of stopping in the dining-room for a Welsh rare bit and a bottle of Apollinaris which they both declared was the very best thing to go to bed upon.

The business of the bells and dog-watches was a fruitful subject for talk. The boys understood it at once, the girls got at it after many explanations; Mrs. Horner did not pretend to understand it, and Miss Augusta asserted that it was useless to try, because " they " changed it so often, a statement Mr. Hervey pronounced unfair, seeing the system was invented by Columbus, and had been used ever since his first voyage without the slightest change.

Tommy was a little puzzled by this, but Philip and Bessie told him afterwards that once for all, he had better believe nothing that either aunt Gus or Mr. Hervey said when they were " chaffing."

" You can believe papa always," said Philip, " and mamma too, only she does not know much."

" And Mr. Hervey," added Bessie, " when he is alone; it is only aunt Gus that makes him tell lies."

The real fact about the bells is that they are planned for the benefit of the sailors, and not for the passengers. The intention is to divide the day of twenty-four hours, into six watches, of four hours each. The bells strike every half-hour, first ONE, then TWO, till they reach EIGHT, which of course takes four hours, and then they begin again. At noon, when eight bells strike, is the time they are most generally noticed by passengers; at half-past twelve, the light stroke is little perceived. Two bells at one o'clock, suggests to many a biscuit, a tumbler of iced champagne and a nap, and so on through the day, each set of bells has an association that long after the voyage is over, comes back with the familiar sound. There are two places, one near each end of the ship, where the bells are struck, so that one set is heard first, then the other, remote and faint like an echo.

So much seems easy to understand, but now comes the dreadful subject of the " dog-watch." The watch means six different sets of sailors who are on duty by turns, for four hours at a time. It would not be fair to have the same set always on duty at night, which is the most disagreeable time, and so they change the order by making two half-watches instead of one long one, between four and eight P. M., thus:

Eight o'clock, P. M. is eight bells.
Midnight, twelve o'clock is eight bells.
Four o'clock, A. M. is eight bells.
Eight o clock, A. M. is eight bells.
Noon, twelve o'clock is eight bells.
Four o'clock, P. M. is eight bells again.

But the sixth watch only lasts two hours, from four to six P. M., and the seventh, also two hours, from six to eight; so as there are only six sets of men the time of watching is uneven, and never the same.

The daily variations of time caused much talk among the children, and indeed the older ones were sometimes puzzled in trying to explain these subjects clearly. Bessie had a little watch which had been given her as a parting present, and as it was her first, she took much pleasure in winding it up and consulting it. She did not like to "jog it ahead" as Jack urged her, half an hour every day, and so it grew more and more behindhand, until it was really easiest to tell time by the bells and verify it by the watch.

"The fact is," she said, "we are cheated out of half an hour every day. To-day we breakfast at nine o'clock and dine at four. Day after to-morrow we shall seem to be doing the same thing, but in reality we breakfast and dine a whole hour sooner. So the day we start we breakfast at nine and dine at four, but the day we get there those hours will be four o'clock in the morning for breakfast, and eleven o'clock for dinner."

"You will have the hours made up for you going home," suggested Miss Lejeune, "then you have to wait half an hour to catch up with the bells and it seems very long."

"Don't speak of going home!" exclaimed Mary gayly. "I wish we were going all round the world in this very steamer."

Her mother groaned gently. Although her ill feelings were over she was not fully reconciled to the motion of the ship; but it was a great pleasure to see Mary so soon recovering her good spirits.

The seat at table next to Bessie was always vacant through the first week of the voyage, but on Sunday, after all were seated, there was quite a little stir in the dining-room as a majestic old lady sailed in, followed by her maid carrying a cushion and wraps. This was the old lady she had noticed before, Mrs. Chevenix, making her nineteenth trip across the Atlantic. She was gorgeously arrayed in a lace cap with scarlet poppies nodding at one side, and a cashmere shawl was drawn over her shoulders. A delicate girlish color, suggestive of rouge, mantled her cheeks, and the light puffed curls on her brow were marvellously black. She was led to the vacant seat by Bessie, and the young Horners gazed at her with awe and amazement. The captain, who spoke but little in general to the others, saluted her with great deference, and she at once began a lively French conversation with him across the table.

"You can leave me, now, Mary," she said to the maid, who had been adjusting the cushion to her back, and a foot-warmer at her feet. "I shall do excellently now. I mean to make an excellent dinner. Everything is sure to be *au meilleur* on a French ship, and *garçon*, tell them to send me a bottle of *vin extraordinaire*."

She looked about graciously upon her companions, and even put up her glasses to scan them more closely, whereupon:

"You have forgotten me, I fear, Mrs. Chevenix; I am Mr. Hervey Mr. Clarence Hervey, of Boston," said that gentleman.

"Ah! my dear sir, not at all; delighted!" replied the old lady. "I should have recognized you at once, but I am so *myope*, you know; absolutely nothing without my glasses."

Mr. Hervey now introduced the Horners, and a great deal of amusing talk followed; for Mrs. Chevenix was still a delightful woman of the world, very agreeable, in spite of her affectations. She told a number of her adventures on previous voyages with great spirit; but alas! before the salad was removed, an unfortunate lurch of the ship was too much for her; she turned pale under her rouge, and moved back hastily, calling:

"Mary! I must have Mary!"

Mary Horner, who was remarkably quick and observant, sprang

forward at once, and half-supporting the old lady with one arm around her, led her quickly to the door of the *salle à manger*, where the faithful maid, who was not far off, received her, and bore her away to her state-room.

After this Mary Horner became a great favorite with Mrs. Chevenix. who soon recovered from this last little attack of sea-sickness, and took her place regularly at meals, entertaining the whole party by her vivacity and shrewd remarks.

Otherwise, they made few intimacies, but many acquaintances on the ship. There was a shy and awkward young man named Buffers, who hovered about the girls a good deal, and finally gained courage to join them in their walks up and down the deck. He had a small moustache, which he fostered much, and a cane with which he was not yet very familiar; but when they came to know him, Bessie did not laugh at him very much, and Mary pronounced him to be a nice boy.

MRS. FREEMAN.

'There was a pretty woman travelling alone, Mrs. Freeman, who received a great many attentions from all the gentlemen on board, until one of them grew so devoted as to drive away all other aspirants. She was said to be a widow, and he was said to be a rich bachelor. It was hoped by all observers that it would be a match, and the assiduities of the gentleman, and the coyness of the lady, were much watched and criticised.

Tommy found several boon companions of his own age, who had

fair to make existence miserable by tearing up and down the stairway, climbing booms, and endangering their lives by hanging over the rail; but the discipline of the ship was strict, and elders were in the majority, so that the nuisance of a horde of ill-disciplined children let loose upon a steamer, was happily escaped. Strange to say there was no boy of Philip's age, which kept him much with his sisters, and in the society of his father's friends.

Thus the voyage drew quietly towards its end; an exceptional passage, every one said, in regard to weather, for they had no storm, and only a few days of drizzling rain. That it had been remarkably pleasant, even Mrs. Horner was willing to allow.

On their approach to France, the question came under discussion, whether they should land at Brest, or go on to Havre. As Miss Lejeune had anticipated, it was easily decided for the latter course. Not only most of the passengers, but the pleasantest ones were to keep on to Havre, and it seemed a pity to break up their agreeable party till the last moment. As it happened, the stop at Brest was made in the middle of the night, a few travelling agents were put on shore in a boat, and the rest saw nothing of the place, but the next day steamed along the channel with a fresh breeze, and some distant glimpses of the rocky coast of northwestern France.

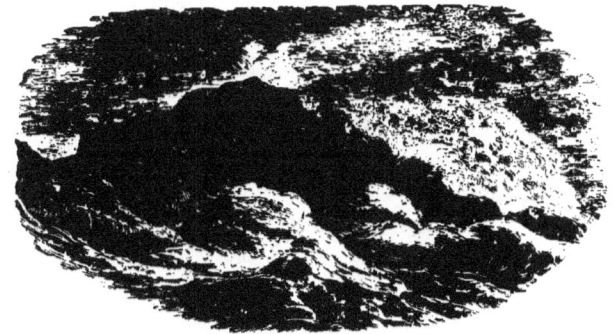

CHAPTER VII.

THE ARRIVAL.

IT was low tide when the *St. Laurent* came to anchor, and it was necessary to land by means of a tug which came alongside of the steamer for that purpose. Being Americans, all the passengers were in a hurry to get off, and each one wished to be the first to leave the ship; they crowded about the gangway long before it was time to go. There was a good deal of wind, and the harbor was full of little waves, which kept the tug bobbing up and down, so that now it was high up above the level of the steamer, and now down below, and it was no easy matter to keep the plank between the vessels steady long enough for the passengers, one by one, to cross.

Our party stood a little aside, watching the exodus with some gloom. Much as she had longed for the end of the ten days and for *terra firma*, Mrs. Horner wished now she need not leave the dear *St. Laurent*, all her fear of the sea returning which had been forgotten during the prosperous voyage. The boys longed to spring upon the tug, and were only kept back by moral and physical suasion. "No hurry," "there is plenty of time," their mentors were obliged to keep saying; they were forced to content themselves with watching those who went before.

Among the rest came dear old Mrs. Chevenix, of whom they had become very fond at last, she was so good-natured, in spite of her little foibles, which they began by laughing at. Mr. Hervey sprang forward through the crowd to help her; she was quite stout and rather blind, and decidedly timid. With the captain, who himself deigned to show her this attention, at one elbow, and Mr. Hervey

THE ARRIVAL.

THE COAST OF NORMANDY.

at the other, and with her excellent maid Mary close at hand, she came to the gang-plank.

"Now, Madam!" said the captain; but before she could advance, down went the tug into a trough of water.

"Wait one moment, Mrs. Chevenix," said Mr. Hervey, as up flew the tug in their faces.

"Now!" "Not yet!" "Now! now!" were the directions following close upon each other, till it seemed as if years went by, before the plucky old lady was deposited in safety on the grimy, smoky little boat, which looked like an impudent little puppy, after their big

Newfoundland of a steamship. The Horners followed close upon Mrs. Chevenix and Mr. Hervey, and the latter, turning quickly as soon as he saw she was safe, succeeded in swinging the ladies across from Mr. Horner, who stood on the steamer. They all joined Mrs. Chevenix, who was in high spirits at her prowess, and very talkative.

"Very polite, that captain, and you too, Mr. Hervey; always trust a Frenchman for gallantry to the ladies; but I told him that was the worst landing I ever made, and he ought to have it attended to. With all the talk about the docks at Havre, it is a pity you can not get into the country without being drowned and breaking your neck. But that is the French all over, they are all for *la gloire.*"

Bessie did not see the connection in these remarks, for she had not paid enough attention to the old lady to understand her style.

The tug went puffing and bobbing on its way, and they could enjoy the sunset light on the water. A packet, crossing the channel from England, swept along, from which the passengers had evidently been watching their late struggle. The people at the bow of the little steamer all looked fresh and in good order, as if the dreaded channel had not kept up its reputation for roughness.

Land was soon reached, but the trials of the party were not yet over. The stone docks are very magnificent, but very steep, especially at low tide; there is a long flight of steps, very damp and slippery at first, built into the stone rampart. It had taken so long to get off the steamer, that it was already growing dark, and very grewsome it was to climb one by one the many steps which led to the top; but at last it was reached. The children, dazed and bewildered with the jargon of a new language, and by the sudden change from their sea life, could hardly now take note of events. Philip said afterwards the only thing he remembered was the queer feeling of a real bed, at the hotel where they passed the night. He felt the motion of the ship more now than at any time since the beginning, and, in fact, it was two or three days before any of them were wholly rid of it.

No time was to be wasted at Havre. Miss Lejeune and Mr. Hervey

ON THE PACKET.

cast longing eyes in the direction of Trouville sur-mer, only about half an hour off, and told the girls some amusing tales of that gay watering place. As the train which they intended to take did not leave till afternoon, a part of the family strolled about the city, saw the statue of St. Pierre, the author of Paul and Virginia, and the many modern, not very interesting, buildings of the handsome town. Far more amusing Philip found it, to look into shop-windows, and to stare at the strong muscular horses, drawing heavy loads.

The first foreign town in one's experience seems very foreign, even

HAVRE FROM A DISTANCE.

if it is cosmopolitan and modern. The commonest sights and sounds of the street are strange and new, and it is these that at first absorb the whole attention. Tommy was amazed and awed. He walked along silently, holding pretty tight to his father's hand.

Tommy did not practice his French in Havre but once, when, left alone with the *garçon*, who was arranging the tray with coffee and eggs in their *salon* in the morning, he said to him rather softly, "*Parlez-vous Français?*"

The waiter did not notice the question at all, he was so busy with spoons and cups, and Tommy was glad he did not, especially when the man, tapping immediately afterwards at the door of Mrs. Horner's room, said with a strong Irish accent:

"Breakfast is ready, mum.'

Everything in the hotel struck them as odd; the windows and doors *à deux battants* opened like folding-doors, never shutting very tight, but with a tremendous clang, with handles like corkscrews, large and clumsy. This waiter was an amazing creature, who climbed countless stairs with a tray on his shoulder, containing coffee and cups and long beams of bread, and *oeufs à la coque*, which was all they were allowed for breakfast. They could have ordered beefsteak and even buckwheat cakes; but this subject had been talked over before, and they all agreed with Miss Lejeune's advice, viz: not to carry their national habits about with them, but to do, in each country, as its inhabitants do. Their life on the French ship had accustomed them somewhat to the plan of a light breakfast. They also prepared themselves manfully for going without iced-water without grumbling, till they reached again the land of Tudor and refrigerators.

Mr. Hervey very simply fell into their party for the present. He joined them in the morning, went with Mr. Horner to look after the luggage at the *Douane*, and, indeed, was of great service, from his knowledge of French and travelling. The French of Mr. Horner, like many another *paterfamilias*, was that of the classics, rather than of daily life. He could recite you pages of Phædre, and was familiar with the *Code Napoléon* in the original, but to call suddenly in French for a bootjack, was beyond him.

It was not long before they were in the train, flying express from Havre to Paris, and, once for all, it may be here described how they usually shook down into their compartment. Mrs. Horner and Miss Lejeune in the seats of honor, the gentlemen opposite them, and the children appropriating the win-

1	2	3	4
1. Mary. 2. Miss Lejune. 3. Mrs. Horner.	4. Tommy. 5. Bessie.	6. Mr. Hervey. 7. Mr. Horner. 8. Jack.	
5	6	7	8

dows. Of course there were changes from time to time in this arrangement.

It worked very well, though not previously planned, that their number just filled a railway carriage; and this they owed, among many nice things, to the addition of Mr. Hervey. There is, to be sure, something to be said on the other side. A large party, filling up one carriage, and always together, is shut out from that contact with other travellers, which is a source of much amusement, and often great pleasure, to a smaller one. But this cannot be helped, and the compensation is being free from the annoyance of disagreeable intruders. On the present occasion, as the train was very full, at a way station a French woman was crowded in upon them, in spite of their number. She was very voluble, and full of apologies. She had a parrot in a

ST. OUEN, ROUEN.

cage in one hand, and she put a basket under the seat, which, she afterwards explained, contained kittens. She would have told her

THE ARRIVAL.

whole history to Miss Lejeune, who was the only person who could understand half what she said, but that another place was found for her by and by, in a "third class," where she belonged.

She left the travellers rather discouraged about their French, but Mr. Hervey assured them that she talked a *patois* that nobody could understand.

With this exception, their whole attention was turned to the scenery from the windows, as the train hurried them along through

ROUEN.

a level, somewhat monotonous, but very pretty country, looking "just like pictures of France," as Bessie observed. Long rows of poplar trees, or willows, and far-stretching fields with neat little houses on them, were all delightfully different from Springfield and Hartford. The trim, well-ordered condition of the road-bed, the tidy little stations, almost always surrounded by neat, bright patches of flowers, enchanted and surprised them; they amused themselves by trying to pronounce the funny names of the stations, as they flew by the white boards on which they were painted. The quiet and method, the absence of hurry, so different from the bustle and confusion of travel in America, even now began to impress them, and to tell upon the nerves of the elders, giving them a feeling of repose, even while in motion.

The trip from Havre to Paris is only five hours, direct, and they had decided not to stop at Rouen and see the cathedral, while resolving to do so later. Many travellers have made this resolution, and failed to come back; but it is not possible to turn aside for every monument on the road, and Paris is a magnet that draws, with a steady pull, those who are set towards it.

ROUEN FROM THE RIVER.

So they contented themselves with the pretty view of Rouen, from the river, as they crossed the Seine.

It was nearly dark, as they drew near Paris, but not enough so to prevent them from seeing everything distinctly, and the sunset light gilded the windows, and spires, and little bits of water, making them sparkle. There was real excitement, which they need not pretend to hide, for all were in harmony, and they had no wish to appear bored or indifferent, as they approached the great capital of the world, which has been so often the centre of human interest. Crossing and recrossing the Seine, they caught glimpses of St. Germain, and saw and heard the names of places they had been reading about all their lives; before they could take it all in, through tunnels and by bridges, and over and under streets they found themselves at a standstill in the gare (or station) of the Rue St. Lazare.

CHAPTER VIII.

DEAR PARIS.

IT was dark; the station appeared vast, strange, and gloomy Our party was hustled, with the rest of the crowd, into an immense dreary barn of a place, where they sat upon a hard bench, to wait for the inspection of the luggage. The gentlemen hovered about near them, at the same time watching their chances of identifying their trunks. The first thing had been to secure outside a small omnibus which would contain them all.

All over Europe the system of baggage checks, used in America, is unknown. Good Americans wonder why it is not introduced universally, and perhaps it will be, one of these days. Meanwhile, at every arrival, it is necessary for each passenger to go and pick out his own pieces. The boxes are all brought and tossed down upon a long sort of counter, pell-mell, as they are in our stations, only a big, separate room is devoted to them, with the hard bench running round it. Each trunk must be identified, and, what is more, inspected by the Custom House officer, and marked with a white cross, in chalk. This inspection does not amount to much, in the case of a long train full of trunks, like the present, and the whole affair passes off more quietly and quickly than might be supposed. "There is no hurry," is the great lesson which Americans begin to learn the moment they go out of their own country.

Twelve trunks to be found and identified, seemed like looking for a whole paper of needles in a hay-stack, in all that mass of big and little luggage; but thanks to the red and yellow bar, and other conspicuous signs, Mr. Horner got his things together, crossed off, and away, in not much more than half an hour, which they were told was surprising luck. Mr. Hervey, meanwhile, had found his own convenient little valise, and they now went to their omnibus, which seemed just a pattern for them. While the tired and timid Horners sat within, the powerful French porters piled the luggage on top of the omnibus, climbing up by a little ladder. As each great trunk crashed down upon the slight roof, they started, and it was indeed an alarming sight to see such a pile upon so apparently slight a foundation. But it appeared to be a mere matter-of-course to the porters; there were, indeed, no Saratogas, and not much sole-leather. So they rattled off at a brisk trot, and heard, for the first time, the click of horses' feet upon the Paris asphalt, driving through the narrow streets to the broad and brilliant *boulevard*, now all lighted

BOULEVARD MONTMARTRE.

with streams of gas, within and without the shops, and columns of electric light. Gaiety, light, movement, are the characteristics of Paris. New York, which follows fast in its footsteps, has not reached yet the air of joyous living which pervades the French city. Even at this hour, people were sitting at the little tables before the *cafés* ordering ices or *absinthe*.

On arriving at Havre, Mr. Horner had found a letter telling him that his rooms were engaged, as he wished, at the Hotel du Rhin, Place Vendôme. He had then only to telegraph the hour of his arrival, in order to be expected at the right time. So now they travelled down the brilliant Rue de la Paix, and round the column to the opposite corner, and under the archway into the odd little court of the ancient hotel.

Here Mr. Hervey left them for the present. He was to put up, much against his will, at the Grand Hotel, on account of a business appointment there. Promising to see them often, without any more definite arrangement, he drove off alone in their omnibus, leaving them to shake down in their new quarters.

WAITER.

The Stuyvesants, who were the chief friends in Paris of the Horners, lived in an apartment in the Rue Joséphine, which is one of the streets of the newer part of Paris, and quite at a distance from the Place Vendôme. But urged by their mentor, Miss Lejeune, the Horners wisely decided to place themselves in the heart of the city, near the shops and theatres, the river and bridges. The hotels are old, and without modern conveniences for the most part, but that in itself makes them more foreign than the modern apartments, which are too much like New York houses to be amusing for their novelty. The older part of the town is more essentially French, and foreign than the other, and therefore "a great deal better fun." So the narrow entry and stairway, rather dirty and not very well lighted, pleased them more than a splendid modern hotel entrance would have done. For that, they should have gone to the Grand Hotel, whose immense courtyards, with wide stairways, elevators, fountains, gilding and mirrors, remind an American of a New York hotel, and fail to give that impression of novelty and antiquity combined, which we ask for in Europe.

So they found themselves soon in a pleasant *salon*, which formed the chief room of their apartment, sitting down to a comfortable little dinner brought to them there. Doors opened from this room, on either side, into bedrooms for Mr. and Mrs. Horner and their daughters. Miss Lejeune appropriated a pleasant bedroom near at hand, although not *en suite*. The boys, to their great glory, were relegated to a room *au cinquième*, by themselves. This was the first time that Tommy had ever gone so far from the maternal wing to roost. Philip good-naturedly consented to look after him, and they went off to bed in great state, followed by the anxious eyes of their mother, who feared something might happen to them in that strange hotel. And thus ended the first whole day of the Horners in a foreign country.

The next morning, when the boys woke up, the first thing that met their ears was the click, click, trot, trot, of the horses' feet in the Place Vendôme, on which their room looked. Suddenly followed a burst of music, from a band in the square. They both sprang from their beds, and ran to look out. Their window, literally in a French roof, was reached by a high step and window-seat, from which they could conveniently look down, far into the place below, and across to the Vendôme column, just before them in the middle of the square.

"My! Is it not just like our paper-weight!" cried Tommy.

The celebrated Vendôme column has been reproduced, in reality, almost as often as it has in miniature for a table ornament. It was originally built by the first Napoleon, to commemorate his victories, in 1803. It was taken down by the Communists in May, 1871; but

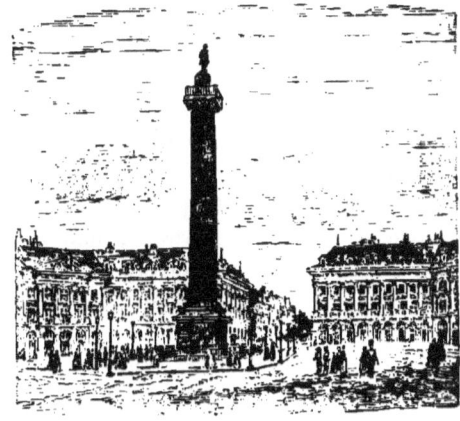

VENDOME COLUMN.

as the fragments were preserved, it has since been again erected.
The statue of Napoleon on top has gone through similar changes. The original one, which he put there himself, made of Russian and Austrian cannons, melted up for the purpose, was taken down by the Royalists in 1814, and the metal employed to cast an equestrian statue of Henry IV. on the Pont Neuf. It was replaced by a monster *fleur-de-lis*, surmounted by a large white flag. In 1831, Louis Philippe caused a new statue of the Emperor to be put on the top of the column, cast of the metal of guns captured at Algiers. This was removed in 1863 to Avenue de Neuilly, and replaced by the present one, representing the Emperor in his imperial robes, and supposed to be just like the original one. The other statue, in the Avenue de Neuilly, was thrown into the Seine by the Communists, in 1871.

Such are the ups and downs of the effigies of the great men of France, as well as their own, and the dynasties they represent. M. Maréchal, the proprietor of the hotel where the Horners were, is said to have offered the Communists five hundred thousand francs, if they would spare the Vendôme column. They said: "Make it a million, and we will see." M. Maréchal kept his money, and the column was destroyed.

The boys were so absorbed, half-dressed with their heads out of window, in watching the lively movement of the street, which was full of little carriages and cabs, the sidewalks crowded with people, gay uniforms, maids with caps, workmen in their blue blouses, and all different from the long lines of busy passengers they were used to in Broadway, that they heard no knock at the door, when their father came to call them, nor his voice, until he crossed the room and put a hand upon the shoulder of each.

"Oh, papa! is it not splendid fun! Can we go down there right off?" cried Tommy.

"Dress yourselves first, and stop for coffee at No. 27," replied his father. "After that you can go out, if Phil will take you."

The boys thought the view from their parlor was less amusing than that they had left, for the windows looked upon the street which leads from the Place Vendôme to the Rue St. Honoré. It is narrow and crowded, and not so gay as the wide square. They found their family, however, refreshed and animated by the sound sleep of the night, and soon Miss Lejeune joined them. The boys were persuaded not to go out till some plan of action had been made for the day; and they were glad of this, by and by, when a tap at the door announced Mr. Hervey, who came thus early to rejoin the party which he had found so attractive hitherto.

"Forgive me," he said, turning to Mr. Horner, "for mentioning the word plans, since you and I are agreed on the two essential rules of travel: First, never to have any; second, never to mention them."

"You are always saying that," exclaimed Philip, rather impatiently, "but I'm sure I do not know what you mean."

"He means, Phil," said his father gravely, "that it is wise in travelling not to allow yourself to be hampered by a plan, made before starting, so much as to lose doing a great many things which may turn up afterwards."

"And then," cried Miss Augusta, "after you have decided to do a thing, do not go and tell everybody, and thus grow tired of your plan before carrying it out."

"However," continued Mr. Horner, "an able general must reveal some plan of battle, I believe, to his troops, before opening the campaign; and I must say I should like to consult with my aids and lieutenants seriously before we advance further. Mrs. Horner thinks," he went on, addressing Mr. Hervey, "that we may as well settle down here for a month or more, before going further, and thus *do up* Paris now. This will accustom us to foreign life, and to the sound, at least, of French; and as we mean to leave the real travelling part till summer, there is no reason for hurrying away from here now."

The young people exchanged glances of delight which was moderated a little as their father went on.

"Miss Lejeune thinks it might be worth while for the girls, at any rate, to take regular French lessons, and perhaps Philip; at all events, we want to have some system in our sight-seeing, and not devour our Paris like a box of *bonbons*. Many people go away with very little idea of the historical monuments of the city; and yet, in that regard alone, it is one of the most interesting places in the world."

The others agreed. Bradshaw and Murray, maps and plans were brought out, and a deliberation seemed about to ensue, when Mr. Hervey, observing the long faces of the younger ones, said, laughing:

"Do not you think they might begin with a nibble at the *bonbon* box? Let every one go out and amuse himself as he likes for to-day. They can not get lost, if they use their Yankee wits."

The grateful children added their entreaty, and, with the condition only that Tommy should keep with one at least of the elders, and with pocket money in moderation, the four youngest members of the party sallied forth from the courtyard of their hotel for their first expedition in brilliant, bewildering Paris.

HOTEL DE VILLE.

CHAPTER IX.

SIGHT-SEEING.

THE result of these deliberations was, that the "famille Horner" were to settle down for a month, at least, in Paris. They soon fell into a certain routine of life which proved very agreeable. Every morning, after the usual cup of coffee and delicious bread and butter, some out-door excursion to "see sights" was made, either in groups or by the whole party, at noon, or later, they lunched at any good restaurant which happened to be in their way; but generally, every one came home to rest or study during the afternoon. At six, or later, a cosy little dinner was served in their own apartment. Two evenings in the week, a French abbé, M. Burin, accomplished, instructed, and agreeable, came to talk French, and to direct the French exercises of May and Bessie, who found time in the afternoons, to write and learn what he gave them to do. He proved so pleasant that every one was glad to join these French conversations, and he soon came to be considered an important member of the family group. His suggestions were most useful as to the direction of their search after objects of interest in and about Paris, and he sometimes went with them to some favorite point of historic or picturesque importance.

The boys were allowed to be free from regular lessons during this time. It may be thought that too little attention was given to study; but Mr. and Mrs. Horner considered that the monuments of Paris, intelligently considered, were in themselves an education for their children, while the language was surrounding them on all sides. In fact, they tried to keep themselves as much as possible in a French atmosphere; and, though careful not to neglect their numerous Ameri-

BRIDGE OF ST. LOUIS.

can friends, they avoided all dinners and invitations of a simply social character. They went often to the theatre, but otherwise stayed at home in the evening: the rest and quiet were most welcome after their active day; and maps and guide-books, volumes of history and reference covered the tables of their pretty salon, and came out every night for consultation.

Mr. Hervey had not been committed to any agreement to stay as long as they did; no one asked him his plans, and he said very little about them. The Horners understood that he had some business, and many friends, to attend to in Paris. Nevertheless, he was not seldom found in their gay little evening-circle, and often joined or led the morning excursion. Boys and girls grew equally fond of him; his presence was felt by all to be an addition, his absence a disappointment.

In the excursions about the streets of Paris, the party seldom went in a body. Sometimes Mr. Horner headed one expedition, Mr. Hervey another. Miss Lejeune was often missing on these, which she called

PLAN OF THE TUILLERIES AND LOUVRE.

rudimentary trips, being, as she said, too familiar with many things to care to repeat; so she spent that time in visiting old friends.

Mrs. Horner saved her strength by resting at home nearly every other day. But Mary and Bessie, Philip and Tommy, were indefatigable sight-seers, and often slipped off a second time in the afternoon. They soon got an insight into the topography of Paris, and could find their way easily, even in the narrow and intricate streets, on the right bank of the river, wherever they found the most interest.

Their first excursion of importance was the walk through the boulevards, so wisely recommended by their beloved Baedeker's Guide. A bird's-eye view of old Paris, which shows the bulwarks as they

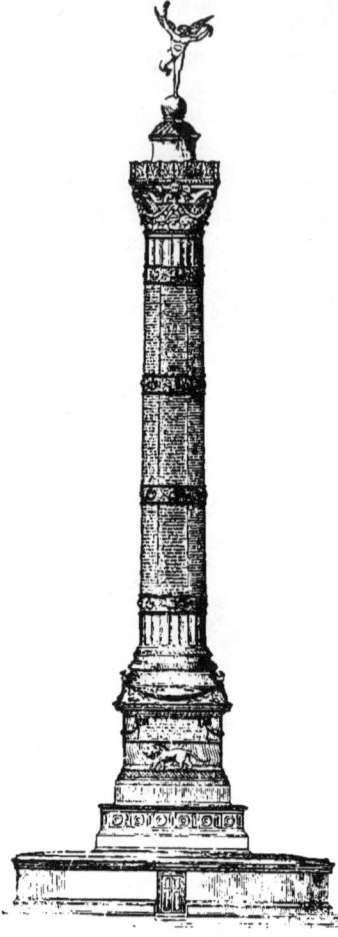

COLONNE DE JUILLET.

looked before the time of Louis XIV., gave them a very good idea of the old limits of the city, and an understanding of how it came to be thus laid out.

In the year 1670, Louis XIV. had these fortifications which then surrounded Paris, removed, and the moats filled up. In their place a line of streets grew up, ever since called boulevards, and these streets are still as gay and brilliant as the newer ones built to rival them. Starting from one end of them at the Place de la Bastille, and walking to the Madeleine, gives a chance to see some of the most striking features of Paris.

The Place de la Bastille itself is interesting as the place where stood the celebrated old prison of which the children had already heard and read. This building was destroyed at the beginning of the Revolution of 1789, and no sign of its gloom remains in the modern column which marks the spot; but it was easy to call up the vision of the dismal old dungeon, where for more than four centuries prisoners of state were shut up, often for no reason at all but some caprice of government. The column of July is erected over the remains of the so-called July Champions, who took part in the revolution of 1830, which made Louis Philippe king. It is of iron, one hundred and fifty-four feet high, with a figure on top of Liberty, holding a

OLD PARIS.

torch and a broken chain. Near by is the place where Archbishop Affré was killed, in 1848, which again was the last stronghold of the Communists, in 1871.

Walking through the streets towards the Madeleine, they become gayer and gayer, the shops larger, with huge windows filled with all sorts of amusing things. The children took up the plan proposed in Miss Ticknor's charming book, *Young Americans in Paris*, which they had all read and liked very much, of trying to see how many of the things in the shops they could name in French as they passed by. Bessie lingered long before a window full of delicious dolls, dressed to represent a wedding. The bride, a fair young blonde doll, was attired in a white satin dress with a long train; she wore a veil with orange blossoms. The little bridegroom stood by her side in irreproachable costume, the parents, the priest, the bridesmaid and "assistants," as the French say, were all there.

As they came through the Place du Chateau d'Eau, a flower-market was going on. The large square was filled with rows of tables heaped with all sorts of flowers from the country, and although it was late in the season, the variety of bright and gay flowers was great. They passed the Grand Opera House, and the Grand Hotel, and came on through the brilliant boulevard des Capucines to the Madeleine.

THE OPERA.

The three older children, Mary, Bessie and Philip, had made this trip by themselves; for with the help of a plan of Paris, they found their way about easily, and they grew to enjoy more and more these excursions of discovery. Things they found out themselves seemed far more important than those which were pointed out to them by experienced elders; and some historical fact, told by a chance old woman in a doorway, became far more real than if they had read it in a guide-book.

They were to meet the elders at a restaurant on the Place de la Madeleine at twelve o'clock. For a wonder, no one was very late, and they had a merry lunch together. Philip, in the hope of becoming a connoisseur in such matters, always studied the bill of fare with great attention, and sometimes ordered a dish purely for the singular name it had; as for instance, *potage à la gibier de l'enfer*. He made

CHURCH OF THE MADELEINE.

in this way, some discoveries of dishes that were excellent; but in general the Horners found it wiser to order "un bon bifstek," or to confine themselves to the dishes which they knew to be solid and good, from their experience on the *St. Laurent*. They believed in good, hearty, nourishing food, and plenty of it; for nothing is so fatiguing as sight-seeing on an empty stomach. Mary was especially sensitive to these physical conditions, as her appetite was still delicate. When she began to be nervous and a little irritable, Philip was in the habit of saying, "Do be quick, and let Mary have something to eat! She is getting cross." People are not enough aware how much amiability of temper depends on a good digestion, caused by regular and wholesome food.

It is an easy and short walk from the Madeleine through the broad and straight Rue Royale to the Place de la Concorde. The Horners especially wished to see the obelisk of Luxor, which stands in the

PLACE DE LA CONCORDE.

middle of that square, to compare it with the one just put up in their own Central Park, in New York.

"How different it looks!" was Tommy's first exclamation, and a true one; for although the obelisk itself is much like the one in New York, the pedestal is different, and the rough corners and the crabs which are such an important feature in the mounting of ours, are wanting. The difference is, however, more in the surroundings of the two. The French one looks slight and elegant, but dwarfed at the same time, in the middle of its square, by fountains and statues and high buildings, and appears less at home than the one in Central Park, standing alone and grand in the midst of simple and natural scenery, away from the noise and bustle of the streets.

The monoliths themselves are very much alike, and the Horner children were pleased to recognize the cartouche of their friend, Ramses II., which they had learned to know at home. The French obelisk was presented to Louis Philippe in 1830, by Mohammed Ali, who was then Pasha of Egypt; in the next year a vessel was sent to bring it home. The task was so difficult that the ship did not return with its costly freight till 1833, and the obelisk was not erected in its present position till 1836. The expenses of the whole undertaking amounted to two millions of francs, and as the obelisk weighs five hundred thousand pounds, it used to be said in Paris that the stone of which it consists, cost four francs per pound.

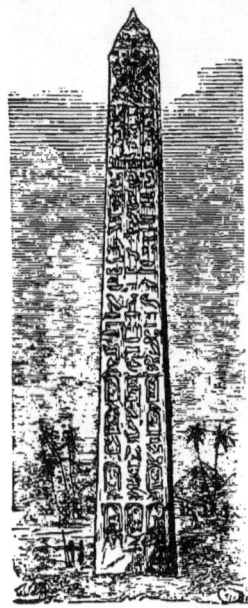
CLEOPATRA'S NEEDLE AT HOME.

While Mr. Horner and the boys, with Bessie, remained in the Place de la Concorde to further recall its historical associations, Mary and her mother, summoning one of the brisk little fiacres which are always to be had at a signal of the hand or parasol, stepped into it and were soon rolling lightly over the asphalt pavement of the Champs Elysées. Miss Lejeune had been standing with them, a little undecided what to do; for an open carriage such as they preferred, only holds two comfortably, though there is a little seat at the back of the driver's box, where a young person like Mary may be precariously wedged in. At that juncture Mr. Hervey was seen rapidly crossing the street towards them, through the many vehicles, horses and passengers that crowd that part of busy Paris. He was looking for the party, knowing it was their plan to meet in the Place at that hour.

"Ah, here you are!" he cried. "I was afraid I should miss you.

LE PARC MONCEAU.

I have been waiting more than an hour for my man with whom I had an appointment for this morning, but as he has not come yet, I determined to cut him."

"How fortunate we did not miss you," said Mrs. Horner; "to meet by chance in Paris seems like looking for a needle in a haymow."

"Cleopatra's needle, mamma, is easier to find than most," remarked Bessie, rather pertly.

The Horners did not snub their parents as much as many American children do, but it sometimes happened.

"We are going to see the Stuyvesants," said Miss Lejeune to Mr. Hervey, "will you walk up with me, and join the others there?"

He smiled. "With pleasure," he replied, "but either they must make a very long call, or we must walk tremendously fast."

"I'll tell you," said Miss Lejeune. "Jeannie, you shall drive round the Arc de l'Etoile and get out and look at it, if you like, which will fill up the time, and we will meet you later at the Stuyvesants."

So it was agreed; the driver received the proper directions, and they separated.

CHAPTER X.

A VISIT.

DOUBTLESS the Champs Elysées is the most beautiful street in the world, it is very wide, sloping gently upward, for a little more than a mile, to the Arch of Triumph, flanked by handsome buildings and planted with elm and lime trees. The first part of it is full of cafés-chantants, juggler's-shows, marionettes, and all sorts of gay entertainments, which make it more amusing to walk than to drive. Nurses in white caps pushing perambulators, little goat-carriages containing happy children, girls with button-bouquets, and a constantly moving mass of passengers fill the broad sidewalks, while the street is crowded with gay equipages, high-stepping horses elegantly harnessed, handsome liveries and gorgeously dressed women; for from two to six are the fashionable hours for driving to the Bois de Boulogne, which is reached by this avenue.

These things so absorbed Mary and her mother that on this occasion they hardly saw the palaces and buildings on their way. Dismissing their little carriage at the Arch of Triumph, they spent some time looking at this graceful and and beautiful monument, called the Arc de l'Etoile, because it stands in the centre of a star of avenues which radiate from it, called boulevards, after the other boulevards, although without the same right to the name.

The first Napoleon meant to erect four triumphal arches in commemoration of his victories. Two, only, have been completed; the one in the Place du Carousel, near the Louvre, by himself, and this one, later, by Louis Philippe. There is a little staircase within the side of the arch, leading to the platform, from which there is a beautiful prospect; but this ascent was postponed for the active legs and easy motion of the boys. Mrs. Horner reserved her strength for the top of the Tower St. Jacques, which gives the best bird's-eye view of Paris, on account of its central position.

TRIUMPHAL ARCH.

The Stuyvesants lived in an apartment directly on the corner of Avenue de la Reine Hortense, with a beautiful view looking directly down the Champs Elysées. Their rooms, to be sure, were *au cinquième*, but the stairs were easy and the situation charming when they reached them, with a little balcony overlooking the street, into which they could look down and watch the carriages and people made small by the distance, and hear the gay trot, trot, of the horses' hoofs on the pavements, and the peculiar cracking of the whips of the Parisian coachmen.

Miss Stuyvesant, the daughter of the house, took Mary out on the balcony, where they rather shyly began an acquaintance, while the mammas conversed within. The ladies were old school-friends, but they had not met for several years, during which time the Stuyvesants had been living in Paris, and had become a part of that large American colony, which stays on year after year, thinking itself on the apex of earthly bliss, but, in fact, having but a dull time of it.

Paris, in the judgment of people like the Horners, is a delightful place to visit for a time, and the best place in the world to study art, or pursue any special object of intellectual culture; but to live in without any such aim, it must be monotonous, at least, for good Americans who are better employed at home in helping the progress of their young country.

Miss Stuyvesant was a pale, rather pretty girl, a little older than Mary, wonderfully well-dressed, with very little to say, after she had asked a great many questions about the voyage, and regretted repeatedly that the Horners were so far down town, a thing she took very much to heart.

Mary was glad when she saw in the distance Miss Lejeune and Mr. Hervey, coming briskly along towards the house. They, of course, were the only people she recognized, though Miss Stuyvesant could tell the names of a number of ladies rolling along in their open carriages, with bright parasols over their heads. Although it was now late in October, the day was warm and sunny.

"Well, that visit is off my mind," said Mrs. Horner with a sigh of relief, when they were in the street again, "although we are in for a dinner there. I begged Mrs. Stuyvesant to postpone it, however, till we are a little more settled."

"Mamma, I think Mr. Stuyvesant is a great deal nicer than the others," said Mary.

"Yes, that is true," her mother replied; "he is an old friend of your father's and he is very fond of him."

"So you did not get on very well with Miss Emily?" asked Mr. Hervey.

"Well, no," said Mary; "it seems as if I had seen more of Paris already than she has, though I have only been here three days."

"Are you tired?" he asked of the ladies in general; "for if not, it would be a nice chance to see the Parc Monceau, which is only a little way off on this street."

These grounds, which formerly belonged to the domain of Monceaux, were bought by the father of Louis Philippe, in 1778, and laid out in a style intended to be entirely novel, differing from both French and English established notions, so as to surprise and delight the

A VISIT.

visitor at every step. Thus the park became at that time one of the most fashionable resorts of the gay world; balls, plays, and fêtes of the most brilliant description were celebrated there.

The Revolution converted the park into national property; at the Restoration it again fell to the house of Orleans, but eventually

PARIS UNDER GROUND.

came into the possession of the city and is now a public promenade; and although not to be compared with the Bois de Boulogne, it has the advantage of being within the precincts of the city. The original fantastic character of the grounds has been to some extent restored, as in the *Naumachie*, an oval sheet of water bounded by a semi-circular Corinthian colonade.

The party were not too tired to spend a little time looking at the rather gaudy, but handsome decorations in the Russian church, which happened to be open on that day, and they then returned to their quiet dinner in their apartment, easily persuading Mr. Hervey to join them.

They found the others still talking of what they had seen; for they had been walking all the afternoon. They crossed the river by the Pont de la Concorde, on leaving that Place, and saw the Hotel des Invalides, the public buildings along the Seine, the Quai Voltaire with its open stalls of old second-hand books, where book-lovers were searching for bargains amongst a mass of apparent rubbish, and so along the river to the island and Notre Dame. Crossing by two bridges they were again back on the upper side; passed the Hotel de Ville, the Tower St. Jacques and the Louvre, with whose façade they were now very familiar, but whose inside treasures were postponed for the present. This was only a sort of preliminary trip, "to get used to the outside of the places," Philip said. They did go, however, to see the tomb of Napoleon, under the dome of the Invalides,

AT THE BOOK-STALLS.

and all of them, even Mr. Horner, climbed to the top of the Tower St. Jacques.

"Three hundred and ten steps, mamma!" cried Tommy, "and you must go up there."

"You really must though, mamma," urged Bessie, "for it is lovely

HOTEL DES INVALIDES.

up there. You can see everything, — the river and the streets, — it is just like a map; and off into the distance the sky and the sunset are splendid."

At dinner they were all talking, more than listening; but every one laughed when Philip was heard to say: "All the places in Paris seem to be scenes of bloodshed, and monuments put up by one man and pulled down by another. I could be a guide to Paris now. All you have to do at each place is to say:

PONT NEUF.

"This was founded by Louis XIV., and destroyed in the Revolution, rivers of blood, &c.; Napoleon I. restored it; Louis Philippe took down everything Napoleon put up. Then Louis Napoleon made an entirely new city of it, and put N on everything, and then the Communists destroyed all, and there were more rivers of blood."

"That is not a bad account of it, Philip," said Mr. Horner gravely, "but you must not get in the habit of thinking lightly of these rivers of blood, although you hear so much of them at every turn. When M. l'abbé comes this evening, who stayed in Paris all through the siege and insurrection, he will tell you that it was no laughing matter to witness those scenes."

"It is a pity that the French have such a passion for destroying their own monuments," said Mr. Hervey. "When I remember how magnificent the Tuilleries, the Hotel de Ville and other buildings were in 1867, at the time of the great Exposition, when Louis Napoleon was at the height of his glory, and then see, as we do now, the workmen still busy restoring the ravages of the Communists, I wonder how long it will be before all is to do over again."

NAPOLEON'S TOMB.

"The French are now building on firm foundations," said Mr. Horner. "I have a good deal of faith in their new republic."

"But only think," said Mary, who had left the table over which the others lingered with nuts and grapes, turning over the leaves of her Baedeker, "how many times the Place de la Concorde has changed its name:

Place Louis Quinze, Place de la Révolution, Place Louis Seize. Place de la Concorde."

"And all the different statues that have been up and down in the middle of it," said Bessie, looking over her sister's shoulder.

"Now that they have this good, inoffensive

TOWER ST. JACQUES.

obelisk there, it may be left unmolested, I hope," said Mrs. Horner.

"But, mamma, they have had a fight there since, in the Communists' times, but 'notwithstanding the violence of the conflict, the obelisk fortunately escaped injury.'"

It was late; Mr. Hervey said good-night, and all retired to sleep soundly.

STEAM TRAMWAY.

CHAPTER XI.

VERSAILLES.

AS the weeks went on, the elder Horners were pleased to find that without a system of study too rigid, the children were beginning to learn something more definite about the history of the country they were in, than they had ever acquired from the books they had read. Paris itself is a record of the alternating periods of splendor and ruin, of which France has been the scene; and in the blank spaces left by monuments destroyed, as well as in those that remain, may be read the changes that have swept over her

In but little more than two centuries has France, and especially Paris, gone through so many reverses, and been the scene of so many triumphs and so much suffering. In 1643, Louis XIV. began to reign, and in 1875 the Republican constitution was *finally* adjusted,—if any importance may be attached to this word. In the meantime the English people have quietly, and, with but little bloodshed, dispossessed their Stuarts, and established the House of Hanover upon the throne; and in the meantime, the United States has been born and grown up to be a lusty and self-asserting member of the company of nations.

It was now the last week in October, but the weather continued soft and lovely, and the Horners availed themselves of it for excursions out of Paris, knowing well that in November such trips would lose their charm. One of the pleasantest of these expeditions was the day they spent in Versailles, which they reached by the tramway, thus getting their first experience of a French steam-horse-car, and coming home by the way of St. Germain, and the ordinary railway.

The children, on arriving, were surprised to find themselves in a town to all intents and purposes as closely built as Paris.

"I thought Versailles was a palace!" exclaimed Tommy, who, as may well be supposed, did not trouble himself with guide-books and histories. He lived for the pleasure of the moment, and although he picked up a great deal of information, it was less from study than observation. His quick eye and sharp little mind helped him to a great many discoveries passed over by his elders.

Versailles is indebted for its magnificence to Louis XIV. It was called by Voltaire *l'abîme des dépenses*, because its palace and park cost the royal treasury a thousand million francs, and to keep it up required every year an immense sum. The palace was the headquarters of his court, and is intimately connected with the history of the period. It witnessed the zenith and the decline of the prosperity of Louis XIV., as well as the life of his successor, Louis XV. The unfortunate Louis XVI. saw the palace sacked by a Parisian mob, and since then it has been uninhabited. During the revolution it narrowly escaped being sold; Napoleon neglected it, and the Bourbons in their restoration merely prevented it from falling to decay. Louis Philippe at length restored the building, and converted part of it into an historical picture gallery.

At Versailles on the 18th of January, 1871, the Prussian monarch, with the consent of the German States, was first saluted as Emperor of Germany. Since the departure of the German troops, in the following March, it has been the French seat of government.

As this was the first palace they had visited, the Horners felt obliged to "do it" pretty thoroughly, and they therefore went through all the rooms which are now open to the public; many of them, being occupied by the government, are not to be seen. It is no small amount of walking which is entailed by this, and by the time they had been over all the parquetted floors, and up and down the stairways leading from one suite of apartments to another, they were all thoroughly tired in spite of the interesting things they had seen; among others, the celebrated *Salle de l'œil de Bœuf*, so called from its oval window, and the bedchamber of Louis XIV., with its furniture now nearly the same as in his time. Miss Lejeune, who had been lately reading the memoirs of St. Simon, gave them an amusing

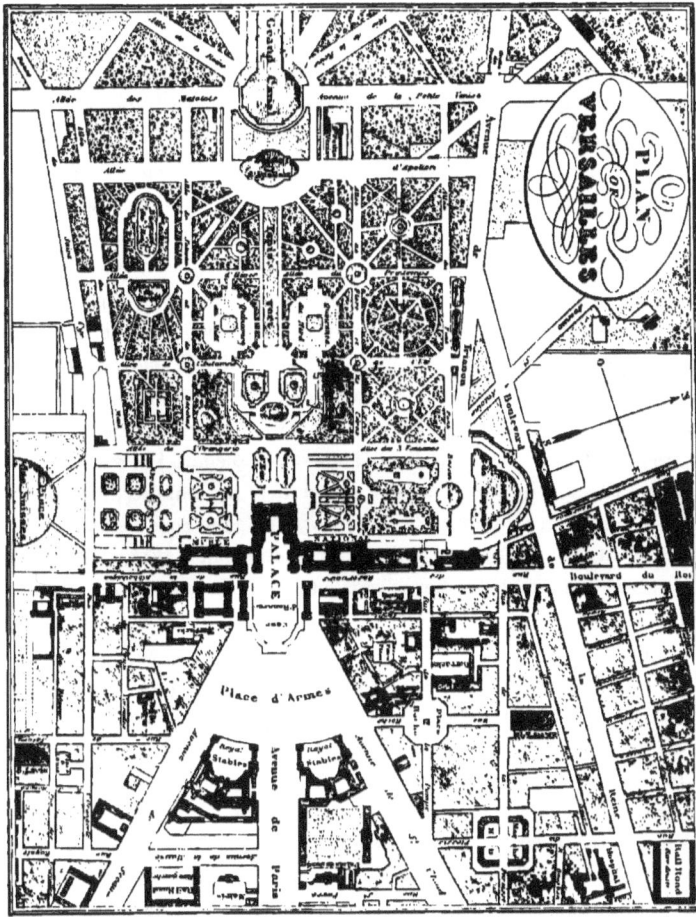

account of the daily habits of the great king. When he got up in the morning, ever so many people, valets, chamberlains and physicians were always present. The chief gentleman gave him his dressing-gown, everybody came in time to find the king putting on his shoes and stockings, which he did himself, " with address and grace." Every other day they saw him shave himself, and he had a little short wig in which he always appeared, even in bed. As soon as he was dressed he kneeled for prayers at the side of his bed, when all the others knelt also, and the captain of the guards came to the balustrade during the prayer, after which the king passed into his cabinet.

As for the picture-gallery, it received very various consideration from the different members of the party. The children studied with interest the sixty-seven portraits of French monarchs, from old Clovis to Napoleon III., and tried to remember how many of them had their heads cut off, and how many died in their beds. The pictures of artistic merit by celebrated painters were those which most interested Miss Lejeune; Mr. Hervey, who cared but little for modern pictures, on account of his affection for the old masters, saw little worth looking at. Mr. Horner, everywhere and anywhere, delighted in any representation of the deeds of the first Napoleon. He was a "*Bonapartiste enragé*," by which is not meant here an admirer, for he considered him an unscrupulous tyrant; but for a long time he had made a specialty of reading all the lives, memoirs, and anecdotes of this celebrated man, and he never missed an opportunity of following him up.

Philip liked all the battle pictures, and Tommy enjoyed looking at a few of them, but he soon pulled his mother away; and, when the rest finally found themselves too tired to understand what they were looking at, they found Mrs. Horner and her younger son seated on the terrace behind the palace, looking out upon the charming, though stiff and formal gardens of Le Nôtre.

He was the most famous landscape gardener of his time. His chief object seems to have been to subject nature to the laws of symmetry, and to practice geometry and architecture upon lawns, trees, and ponds. But the quaint, solemn, old-fashioned look of the grounds is in harmony with the architecture of the palace, and is a good example of the notions of art which prevailed in the time of Louis XIV.

Our party assembled to rest and chat on one of the benches near the *tapis vert*,— a long lawn below the wide steps leading from the palace. It is very pretty, and on this lovely, warm October day

VERSAILLES.

was full of charm. The leaves were already falling; dried ones were floating about, and dropping on the green grass.

"What a pretty name," said Mary, repeating it; "*tapis vert!*"

"You would not think 'green carpet' such a very romantic name," said Philip, who was lying flat upon it, with his heels in the air, having noted the absence for the moment of every form of policeman.

GARDEN LAID OUT BY LE NÔTRE.

"No, that's it," said Mary; "the French language makes everything pretty, just as all their things are pretty. I think they are a pretty people."

"A very pretty people, I should say they were," rejoined Phil, "to take so much pleasure in destroying all their own monuments."

Miss Lejeune was very desirous to drive to Marly and St. Germain, after the manner so often described by her beloved St. Simon as the frequent excursion of Louis XIV. and his court. As Mrs. Horner was tired, she decided not to attempt this; and after their hearty and well earned lunch at a restaurant outside the palace grounds, she went back to Paris by rail with Tommy, while the rest joined Miss Augusta. They were glad they did so, for the drive having rested, and the lunch refreshed them, they were able to see all they cared to of St. Germain, its château and town, and to stroll in the beautiful forest. It was

CHATEAU OF ST. GERMAIN.

here that James II. of England, exiled from his country, lived for twelve years and died, while Louis XIV., who was born here, was building and improving Versailles. Louis grew tired of the cost and bustle of Versailles, however, and, persuading himself that he should like something quiet and solitary, he hit upon Marly, between the two places; and beginning with the idea of having no expense whatever, he spent more money upon it than even at Versailles.

ROBERT DE COTTE. ARCHITECT OF LOUIS XIV.

chiefly in clumsy great machines to bring water to the latter place. Building and changing his plans, were the great delight of this funny old King Louis XIV.: to put up and pull down, to arrange and then alter, was

'—— the chief of his diet,
and yet this old monarch could never be quiet.'

114   A FAMILY FLIGHT.

The Horners talked and read so much about him, that he grew to be an intimate friend. His portraits at Versailles and at the Louvre made him familiar to them. It is said that he invented high heels, to make himself look tall and dignified, but he must have been really fine-looking; and, when he was "got up" in his flowing wig, velvets, embroideries, and laces, was, doubtless, an imposing figure. He was a wonderful man; for it must not be forgotten that his water-works and his carp-basins were not the only things which occupied his mind. Great wars, and great victories, too, throughout his reign, were due to his determination and energy. The contest with England and her allies, which lasted so long, and in which the victory was often on the side of France, in spite of the triumphs of Marlborough and Prince Eugéne, who fought against Louis, was owing, as much

STATE EQUIPAGE.

as to any other cause, to the persistent friendship of Louis to the exiled Stuarts. When a battle was taking place near at hand, he would get into his immense old-fashioned coach, with half a dozen ladies, and drive out to see how the fighting was going on. In the coach, during these journeys, there were always all sorts of things to eat, such as meat, pastry, and fruit, and the king was always urging his companions to eat, although he did not himself.

The Horners saw some huge coaches at the Little Trianon, which is a part of Versailles, and amused themselves with fancying the royal party seated in one of them, and having to eat when they were not hungry, because the king wished them to.

Louis employed many architects, one of whom was Robert de Cotte, of whom Rigaud, a portrait-painter of the time, made a fine picture which gives a good idea of the costume of the time.

Louis XIV. reigned from 1643 to 1715.

NOTRE DAME.

CHAPTER XII.

TOMMY'S LARK.

WHILE the others were thus following the fortunes and reviewing the character of *le grand monarche*, Mrs. Horner and Tommy were not without their little adventure.

In their compartment of the train going back to Paris, who should they find but Mr. Stuyvesant, who had been to Versailles, not as a pleasure-trip, but on a matter of business. He was what the children called a very jolly man; very different from his family, they thought. He now proposed to Mrs. Horner the plan of stopping at Sévres, in order to walk across the pretty park of St. Cloud, and there to take a steamboat back to Paris, on the river. Tommy's eyes sparkled; his lunch had restored the natural activity which had been taken out of him by the long walk through the galleries at Versailles, and he was rather gloomy at the thought of settling down to pass the afternoon in the Hôtel du Rhin. But Mrs. Horner was really tired; so she said:

"I think, if you don't mind taking Tommy, I will go home alone. Mr. Horner has given us such careful directions I am not afraid; it is only to take a cab at the station."

At this moment the train whizzed up to the Sévres station; there was no time to discuss the matter, and Mr. Stuyvesant and Tommy jumped out. Just then, a gentleman was springing into the compartment they were leaving, who bowed to Mr. Stuyvesant.

"Ah, Monsieur! allow me to recommend to you my friend, Mrs. Horner, *une Américaine* who goes quite unattended to Paris."

The door banged, the train swept off, leaving Mrs. Horner a little embarrassed at finding herself alone with a strange Frenchman, whose name, even, she had been unable to catch.

She was a good deal chaffed about this adventure by her family afterwards. The gentleman, M. Rohan-Condé, proved very polite, and, although he did not speak a word of English, succeeded in understanding her French, though Philip was in the habit of describing it as only rudimentary. He pointed out to her the many objects of interest on the route, and, on their arrival in Paris, not only found a cab, but insisted on driving with her to the door of the hotel, where he left her raising his hat with the most elegant of bows, and the most fervent expressions of gratitude for being allowed to protect her.

Mrs. Horner shut herself up in her room for a nap, rejoicing in the exceeding quiet of the empty apartment. Just in time for dinner, the others arrived, tired, but in the best of spirits, Mr. Hervey with them; but where was Tommy? Dinner was served, and yet he did not come. Mrs. Horner now reproached herself seriously for losing sight of him. The gentlemen urged her not to worry, and constantly repeated their assurance that all was right; but a little feeling of doubt hung over the party, till between eight and nine, when the door flew open with a bang, and Master Tommy appeared alone, in a state of noisy triumph after his expedition.

"Well!" cried the girls; "where did you come from?"

"Where is Mr. Stuyvesant?" asked the father of the family.

"He just left me at the door," replied Tommy; adding with an air of great consequence, "we have been dining at Véfour's."

Everyone shouted. Véfour's is a luxurious restaurant in the Palais Royal.

Mrs. Horner wanted to embrace her prodigal little son, but he broke from her, so full was he of his adventures.

"And it is splendid in the evening, all sparkling and glittering with shops, and diamonds, and jewelry. See what Mr. Stuyvesant bought me."

It was a ridiculous little cane, with a gilt top, like those carried by gentlemen, but adapted to Tommy's size.

"You are not hungry then, I suppose?" asked the still anxious mamma.

"No, but I do not mind a few more nuts," replied Tommy, transferring a handful of almonds to his pocket.

"You see," he explained, "we did not stop at Sèvres, but walked right along through the Park of St. Cloud to the top of a place where there is a splendid view. Mr. Stuyvesant bought us some *gaufres*, they are a superior kind of waffle. You can see Paris, and the Arch of Triumph, and the Invalides, and the river, all covered with boats and business. It was hot there, in the sun. You ought

AT ST. CLOUD.

to have seen a man who wanted to sit down on a bench that had just been painted.

"I was afraid we should have to go all over another palace, for my legs ached still, from Versailles; but luckily it is all pulled down, so we did not have to do that, only look at the views; and then we went down to the quai, and luckily there was a steamboat, for they have stopped running, only this is some kind of a feast-day; and so it came along, and it is the greatest thing we have done yet, to see all the people jabbering French on board, and the little tugs and things snorting about on the river. Then going under the bridges! And I saw a great many principal buildings on the banks, which Mr. Stuyvesant explained to me."

"Stuyvesant," corrected Philip.

"Well, Stuysevant," repeated Tommy. "Well, when we got to the place to land, it was after six, and we thought it was better to take our dinner at Véfour's, before coming on up here"

"You should have told Mr. Stuyvesant that your mamma would be worried," said Mr. Horner, in mild reproof.

"I did, papa, I did, really; but to be sure I did not think of it till we got to the ice-cream. Then he said that he had been thinking of that, but he hoped we should not be very late, and that you would excuse us, just this once."

"Well, go now to bed, for it is long past your bed-time," said his mother. "You will want to be well rested before to-morrow, for we are thinking of making an early start for the Louvre."

"What! another palace, so soon?" groaned Tommy.

They shut the door upon him, and he scrambled off up the stairs to his bedroom *au cinquième*.

St. Cloud is named after St. Chlodoald, the grandson of Clovis, who founded a monastery there. It is just near enough to Paris to have been the scene of many a battle in the mediæval contests. Henri III., when besieging Paris in 1589, pitched his camp at. St. Cloud, and was assassinated there by Jacques Clement. The palace, now a ruin, was built by a wealthy citizen in 1572. It was bought and rebuilt by Louis XIV., who presented it to his brother, the Duke of Orleans. In 1782, it was purchased by Louis XVI., for Marie Antoinette.

It was a favorite resort of the first Napoleon, and afterwards became the principal summer residence of Napoleon III.

In October, 1870, the château, the barracks near it, and many of the houses in the town, were completely burned down No town in the environs of Paris suffered so severely in the Prussian war, or presented so melancholy an appearance after it. For two years or more, the streets were a chaotic mass of ruins; but many of them have since been rebuilt, though the château has not been yet restored.

The attraction of the place is, therefore, the park, laid out by Le Nôtre, in the same stiff fashion as Versailles, and the beautiful view of the river and the city beyond, which Tommy enjoyed while he was eating his cakes.

After this, Mr. Stuyvesant and Tommy became very intimate. When Mr. Horner had convinced himself that his old friend really

OUTSIDE THE PALAIS BOURBON.

liked the boy, and did not suffer himself to be imposed upon by him, he was only too glad to lend Tommy for excursions about Paris; and thus he came to see things which the others missed, and of which he afterward boasted to the end of time.

He was with Mr. Stuyvesant one day in the beginning of November, when the members of the legislative assembly were gathering at the Palais Bourbon; and Mr. Stuyvesant pointed out to him M. Gambetta, now the leading man in French politics, toward whom the world was then looking in wonder whether he would favor a time of tranquil

M. GAMBETTA.

republicanism for France, or if he might be plotting a *coup d'état*.

He took him to the Bourse, in the very height of its business-hour; and here he saw from the gallery the *corbeille*, as it is called, where brokers of the stock exchange were gathered in an immense crowd. The noise, the bawling, and excited gestures of the speculators were wonderful to Tommy, although it was almost frightening; the only intelligible words amidst the din were: *"je donne! je prends! je vends!"*

The others saw the busy scene from the outside; but it was only Tommy, who penetrated, with his experienced guide, to the very heart of it.

OUTSIDE OF THE BOURSE.

CHAPTER XIII.

THE LOUVRE.

IT was not according to the Horners' system to do up the Louvre as many tourists are obliged to, in one long, fatiguing tour of inspection. Their day at Versailles would have taught them how unsatisfactory this sort of sight-seeing is, if they had not known it before. Staying, as they did, more than a month in Paris, they had plenty of time to go again and again to the palace, and as their hotel was not far from it, they rather often made the Louvre their place of meeting.

In general, walking through any museum, without a special object, is the most tiresome thing in the world; tiresome to eyes, brain, and legs. The intelligence soon refuses to take any note of the objects seen, and the process becomes a mechanical advance from corridor to gallery. Practiced travellers acquire a knack of passing rapidly through a collection of pictures, or of curiosities, and with a catalogue and a few well-thrown glances, they manage to pick up a vague idea of the things shown; but to do this, some previous knowledge of their nature is necessary.

Mr. Horner was careful to induce the children to have some special object of interest each time they went to the Louvre. Their plan

LOUVRE.

PICTURE IN THE LOUVRE.

was, to study thoroughly one part of it at once, and no other; not to stay very long, above all, not long enough to get tired and hungry.

In this way, they never came to consider the Louvre such a bore as Miss Stuyvesant had described it to Mary on her first visit, though Tommy's countenance sometimes fell, when he found the Louvre was made the programme for the day.

Thus the pictures, the statues, the Egyptian collection, etc., were all taken separately at different times, and recurred to afterwards, according to the inclination of different members of the family. The Egyptian antiquities were very attractive to every one of the party, and if they spent less time there than they would have liked, it was because other things seemed more pressing, and they all combined to form a plan, or a vision, rather than a plan, of going up the Nile sometime, to see for themselves the Ramses family at home.

Miss Lejeune had a fair knowledge of the history of art, and of the merits of pictures ancient and modern. She thought Mary was old enough to be interested in the fascinating subject, and, indeed, at school the year before, Mary had been pretty well grounded in the early schools of art, by a course of lectures illustrated by photographs of the pictures of the oldest masters. She had with her the little note book she had made containing dates of the lives of the Bellinis, Carpaccio, and others of the early Venetian school, to which the lectures had been chiefly devoted; and she was now interested in finding all the examples of their work she could, to see whether she could recognize them by her recollection of the photographs. This excellent preparation made her enjoy many old pictures which Bessie did not hesitate to declare horrid old things. Mary and Miss Lejeune got but little sympathy for their preraphaelite tendencies, and therefore went by themselves, whenever they made a pilgrimage to the shrine of ancient art.

It is a study which grows with exercise. Mary soon began to wish that the gallery of the Louvre contained more old pictures, and to hope that their tour would take them to towns where these are to be seen at their best. Miss Lejeune told her that at Berlin, and Dresden, and also at London, on their way home, they should have a chance to see some of the most celebrated works of the old masters; though

Florence, Venice, and Rome, where the best are, must be left for another trip, and Spain also. There are enough examples of the works of the most celebrated masters of art at the Louvre, to satisfy a beginner, at least. Miss Lejeune was delighted to find that Mary was willing really to study these pictures, and to compare the characteristics of different artists. To her own surprise, Mary found she was soon able to recognize a Fra Angelico, or a Bellini, and guess pretty nearly, if not always right, the school of painting to which a picture belonged. The early Venetian pictures, for instance, she came to know by their rich coloring, as well as by the grave simplicity of the subjects. A Raphael she could soon recognize at the first glance. As for Peter Paul Reuben, as Philip disrespectfully called him, they all soon became familiar with his positive reds, blues, and yellows; his blowzy Marie de Médicis, surrounded by fat angels. The girls found them delightful to follow, in connection with the history of

PALACE OF THE LUXEMBOURG.

this poor queen, driven out of her country by a managing cardinal, just when she had made her palace, the Luxembourg, luxurious to live in.

PALAIS ROYAL. VIEW FROM THE SQUARE.

PALAIS ROYAL. VIEW FROM THE GARDEN.

127

There are twenty-one large pictures of scenes from her life, ordered by her from Rubens. He made the original sketches for them which are now at Munich; for the Louvre pictures are chiefly the work of his pupils, executed under his direction. The mixture of history and allegory in them seems absurd, and Rubens' ideal of feminine beauty is too fat and florid to please all; but the series serves to show the events of the life of their heroine in an entertaining manner. Seeing Henry IV. in the character of Jupiter, and Mary de Médicis in that of Juno, larger than life and twice as blooming, made them remember better than learning it in a chronological table, that Henry IV. and Mary de Médicis were husband and wife.

Miss Lejeune begged Mary to reserve her judgment of Rubens as a great master till she should see his finest work at Antwerp; and meanwhile, to think of him not only as a painter of stout women, but a great traveller and accomplished gentleman, and a good friend to the exiled queen, who finally died at his house in Cologne.

The pictures of their friend, Louis XIV., and of the people of his time, they sought out upon the walls, wherever they could find them, by Rubens, by Rigaud, and by Vandyck, whose portraits are unrivalled in the world.

On the whole, before they left Paris, Mr. Hervey and Miss Lejeune were satisfied in feeling that their young friends were beginning to know how to look at pictures, which was all they hoped for, in these early days. They had found out that a gallery is not like a shop window, where you may stare, admire, pass on, if you like, or stop and buy what you please; but a place to be approached in reverence, and with the acknowledgment of ignorance.

"That's pretty!" "that's horrid!" "I don't think much of that!" were the criticisms they heard one day in the Salon Carré of the Louvre, from two young persons with a strong American accent, one of them nibbling from a box of sugar-plums, the other hopelessly lost in her catalogue. The Salon Carré contains the gems of the collection, and a few of the most celebrated pictures in the world. It would be well, if, instead of judging at a glance of these pictures, as of a piece of cambric on a counter, these young women had tried to think

LANDSCAPE IN THE LOUVRE.

why they were world-renowned, and to weigh the importance of the judgment of several centuries against their own flippant taste. This would have helped them to an interest in the pictures and subjects, and perhaps after they had looked a little into the intention of the artists, their methods, their lives, and the causes of their fame, they would find their own opinions modified, and without affectation would be able to detect beauty and marvellous skill where they at first had seen but a daub.

The Horners did not ask for their children a precocious perception

GUIDO'S SAINT SEBASTIAN.

of the excellence of good pictures. They wished them to know, however, what is a really correct standard of taste in these matters,

BY ALMA TADEMA.

and to feel that if they differed from this, it was a defect in their judgment, and not the blunder of the world's verdict.

They all found pictures which they liked, not on account of being marked with a star in Baedeker, or attached to a famous name; such as charming landscapes, the triumph of the modern French school, realistic reproductions of classic scenes, in which Alma Tadema excels, and many others.

IN AN OMNIBUS.

To linger over the treasures in the Louvre, would fill up our book, and take the Horners but one step on their year's trip. Their month in Paris was too short to do these collections full justice, and especially

THE LOUVRE.

OLD COURT-YARD.

as they had so many other things to fill up their time and attention.
Their interest in Marie de Médicis, which the Rubens pictures had increased, made the Horners ready for the Palais du Luxembourg, and here they saw some more modern pictures. The day they devoted to this gallery, Tommy was rewarded for his general good behavior

of late, on such occasions, by a long excursion in an omnibus with his father, in that part of Paris on the left bank of the Seine, generally spoken of as the other side of the river, although it occupies as much as a third of the city, and is full of objects of interest. The streets are, for the most part, old and narrow, sometimes with openings into quiet old courts, as remote and tranquil as if the bustle of the boulevards was in another world.

This expedition wound up with a visit to the Jardin des plantes, where Tommy was never tired of watching the monkeys, with their friendly cats domesticated among them, and "Martin," the bear, who seemed to understand French as well as, or better, than he did himself. Later in their travels Tommy had a chance to make acquaintance with Martin's relations.

Another day Mr. Stuyvesant, who took every chance to improve his intimacy with Tommy, gave him a delightful tour in the Bois de Boulogne, and all about the Jardin d'acclimatation, which is another collection of animals scattered about in the open air, with all their natural surroundings, as far as possible.

CHAPTER XIV.

LAST DAYS IN PARIS.

IT would be in vain to detail all the things our friends, the Horners, saw and did during their month in Paris. As the difficulty was then to select what to see and what to neglect, so it is now what to describe that they did see, and what to omit. At first the visit before them seemed so long, they thought, even the wisest of them, that there would be time for everything. As they found out more and more what was to be done, the days seemed too short, and their strength inadequate for their sight-seeing, without falling into a senseless, mechanical routine of going from one museum to another, checking them off as they went in their guide-books.

THE LEADER.

They went several times to the theatre, especially to the Théatre Français, although Sara Bernhardt had already left that stage, and was probably, at that time, superintending the marvellous costumes with which she was to astonish the American world. At first the young people could not enjoy the play much, but as they became more accustomed to using and hearing French all the time, the meaning of it all seemed to open upon their ears, and before they left Paris, they listened, almost as to an English performance, and could now recognize the stately pronunciation and careful diction which is insisted upon at this classical theatre.

Two Sundays, in the afternoon, Miss Lejeune went to Pas-de-loup concerts, by the orchestra celebrated under the name of this leader. Mr. Hervey from the first confessed himself unmusical, but this defect was, though unwillingly, condoned, on account of his great excellence in other particulars. Mary and Bessie both enjoyed music, without having, either of them, talent enough to cultivate by taking lessons. The different churches and cathedrals were visited in turn, and they heard, one Sunday, the military mass at the Invalides.

Mr. and Mrs. Horner were not able to avoid a few dinners and evenings given them by their American friends. A dinner at a boulevard restaurant, which genial Mr. Stuyvesant insisted upon giving, was a very gay affair.

MISS STUYVESANT.

Miss Lejeune had many friends in Paris, and was constantly meeting acquaintances of former visits to Europe. But she managed to keep with her party almost always.

"You see, my dear," she said one day, to a charming little French lady with whom she had once spent a month at Nice, "you see I am here this time with a purpose. These Horner children must be educated."

"I see, *ma chère*," replied the countess, "that among you all, you will make prigs of them. Who ever heard of taking our dear Paris

LAST DAYS IN PARIS.

au sérieux to such an extent! Even the Communists made a joke of it, when they were knocking down our best buildings. I declare, I felt sorry for those two pretty girls you were drilling in the Louvre the other day, you and your *beau jeune homme*."

"Don't be afraid," laughed Miss Augusta. "If our adventures should be written, I am sure there would not prove to be too much system in them. But we really wish our young people to leave Paris not without a few ideas."

"Ideas!" exclaimed Madame de Mersac, "if that were all. I am afraid, however, that they will suffer from a real indigestion of facts!"

"Heaven forbid!" uttered Miss Lejeune, and they parted, for it was in a shop, and each had an engagement.

Miss Lejeune would have thought the education of the girls very ill-conducted without some practice in intelligent shopping in Paris, not only at the gorgeous magazines of the boulevard, but the wonderful intricacies of the Bon Marché, and the *Printemps*; the latter, alas! burned down since the Horners saw it; but doubtless, like the natural spring, to blossom forth again.

The Bon Marché is an immense warehouse like Macy's in New York, "only more so," as Philip said. It is a little world in itself, where everything buyable may be found. The people who sell are

ON THE BOULEVARD.

assiduous and affable, and not aggressive, which makes shopping easier than it is sometimes found to be in New York and Boston.

Mary, who was left one day with Bessie at a counter trying on gloves, rejoiced to practice her sprouting French with the clerk who showed them to her. She talked more than the occasion really required, for she thought she was getting on pretty well, and that it was a good chance to pass herself off as a real Parisian. She imitated, as well as she could, the man's accent, and reproduced his terms of expression in her own sentences. When the business was over, which took some time, for she and Bessie were each buying a dozen to take away with them, the clerk said, in the best of English:

"Shall I send these for you? You are staying, I believe, at the Hôtel du Rhin."

Mary stared at him, amazed and mortified, and at the same time afraid the man might mean an impertinence, but he came from the State of Maine, had been a clerk at Arnold and Constable's, in New York, and knew her mother by sight perfectly well. He had seen them all once or twice at different public places in Paris, and thus, with republican familiarity, ventured to scrape acquaintance.

Mary took it good-naturedly, but as Bessie told the story afterward, it caused a general laugh at the expense of Mary's French.

Perhaps the pleasantest part of the Paris period, as the Horners looked back upon it, was the quiet evenings at home in their salon at the hotel, when, resisting theatres, concerts, restaurants, and invitations, they settled down about their moderateur lamp and round table, to talk over the events of the day, with the pleasant French abbé, and, as the case might be, Mr. Stuyvesant, Mr. Hervey, or others dropping in. Not a few agreeable people had discovered the charm of this intelligent little family circle, and the only regret attaching to it was, that it was not permanent in Paris.

One evening Miss Lejeune was repeating her little conversation with the French countess, whereupon Mr. Horner said:

"Well, children, come now, do you suppose we really have learned anything?"

"Of course we have!" mumbled Tommy very sleepily, from a

corner of the sofa where he had been dozing, with his head jammed up against his mother.

"I think we have learned," remarked Mary, "that there is a great deal to learn."

"And I think," said Philip, "that we have found out how and where to find out more about the things we do not know."

"Yes," said Bessie, who was knitting a long and mysterious thing, a feeble imitation of Miss Augusta's everlasting stripe, "if we do not forget to find them out afterward."

"I think it would be a good plan for all of us," said Mrs. Horner, "when we get to some quieter place, to write out our impressions of all the things we have seen in Paris."

"Do you think, mamma," said Philip, coming to take the place by her side, which Tommy had reluctantly left to go to bed, "do you think we shall ever get to a quieter place, until we get home? There will always be a museum, or something."

"Tell me now, Phil," said Mary, lightly, "before you fall asleep, who was Marie de Médicis?"

"Second wife of Henri IV.," replied Philip, promptly, "mother of Louis XIII., grandmother of Louis XIV.: poor old queen who quarreled with Richelieu and got turned out of France, made a great deal of trouble, and died in the Pays-bas."

"Good for you!" continued Bessie, "and Louis XV. was great-grandson of Louis XIV., because the other heirs to the throne kept dying between, and Louis XIV. would live forever; and then by the time Louis XVI. came to the throne, the money was all spent, and the splendor was all gone, and the people rose up and guillotined all the royal family, and that was the end of the great house of Bourbon."

"Oh no! you forget Louis XVIII., and—"

"No," said Bessie, very positively, "because that I do not count. After the revolution, comes Bonaparte, and then with a little gap of republics and trifling kings, Louis Napoleon, with the second empire."

"You would do well, my dear, at your leisure to look up your gap and your trifling kings," remarked Miss Lejeune, "for they are really not without importance."

The abbé, who understood English very well, was laughing at this summary fashion by which his country's history was disposed of.

"If you had lived through all that gap, Miss Bessie, you would not think it so trifling."

"Oh, I did not mind that," said Bessie hastily, and coloring, "only these other times seem more like landmarks to fix dates to."

The old abbé patted her shoulder lightly.

"You do very well, my young Miss, to have so any an idea of my monarchs."

"Papa is the man for Napoleon," cried Philip. "He and I went all over the Invalides, which the rest of you have not yet, and I believe papa has seen every relic of him that can be found in Paris."

"Yes," said Mr. Hervey, "while the rest have been otherwise occupied, you two have been working up your Bonapartes, I believe, thoroughly."

"After I got Abbot's history of him out of my head," said Philip, "I could begin to enjoy his battles and his ambition. But that is so flattering, full of accounts of his magnanimity, and giving crowns to small boys—"

"You mean taking crowns from large kings," said Mary.

"Oh pshaw, Mary!" exclaimed Philip. "I mean a lot of anecdotes about his clemency, illustrated by cuts."

"I believe," said Mr. Horner, "those florid histories of Napoleon which were written at first, really injured his glory by giving a false account of him. The more I read of him, and the feats of his tremendous will, as well as his weak and mean traits, the more remarkable he appears."

It was now late in November. The weather had been unusually mild for Paris, but of late, the days were chilly and raw, so that the Horners had a fire in their salon. But the stupid little French grate has no power, apparently, for giving out heat. The dull coals glowed, but warmed not; Philip pulled up and down the blower attached to the fire-place in vain; they all shivered, even when close to the hearth. The very day after this last conversation when they woke up, the streets were white with snow! A brisk flurry **was**

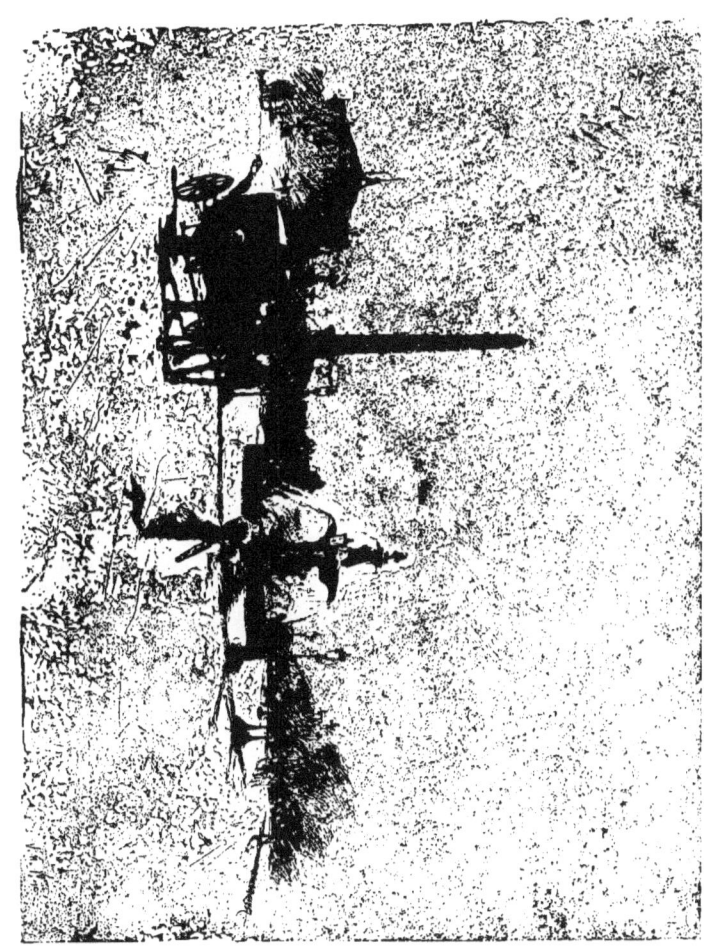

SOWING.

falling on the fountains and the obelisk in the Place de la Concorde

It was a warning that they had stayed long enough. Paris in winter, in a hotel, is uncomfortable, and it was their plan (if they had any) to settle in Germany for the short months of the year, and especially, to spend Christmas in some essentially German town.

In a few days their establishment was broken up, their trunks were packed, and they were actually over the border. Mr. Hervey accompanied them to the station and saw them finally off, promising, however. to meet them somewhere soon.

And so with infinite regret they were leaving their dear Paris, and their pretty French language, to become Germans!

FRENCH ROOFS.

CHAPTER XV.

OUT OF FRANCE.

OUR travellers were now for the first time to be put to the severe test of a long, unbroken railway journey of hours, riding night and day until they should reach Frankfort.

There are evidently two opposite plans of travelling, which might be called the "kill-yourself-but-get-there," and the "take-it-easy" systems. If the first of these is adopted, an immense amount of ground may be covered in a short time. Tourists, on the continent, are at all times to be met, with their guide-books at their noses, and their Hendschel's railway-guide ever open before them, rushing by express-train from one large town to another, doing in each its cathedral and checking off its gallery, and then off and away for the next.

The natural result of this method is, that the tourists who employ it fill their heads with the names of towns, routes, and countries. They show a remarkable power of remembering where they have been, but a feeble recollection of what they have seen.

The take-it-easy plan, as it sounds, is more comfortable, and more improving. The take-it-easy people are far more entertaining about their travels, although in talking with the other sort they are frequently tripped up by the question:

"Did you go to so-and-so? No? oh! you ought not to have missed that! Why, it is the only place on that route worth seeing. Let me see; what was it we saw there? oh, the cathedral, of course. What! no cathedral? no, to be sure; it was a bear we saw there."

Still, there are faults in the take-it-easy plan. It must be admitted that in the fable of the hare and the tortoise, the hare got over the most ground in a given time, and life is too short for the tortoise business nowadays.

Some experienced travellers, therefore, believe in a judicious combination of the two plans, and their way is to stay and rest, observe, and learn in some important place, and then to take great swoops, even across continents if necessary, in express-trains, regardless of fatigue, in order to alight in the next place they wish to thoroughly examine.

It was now well on in December, and the season was too late for attractive study of nature. This was no time for the Rhine, or for short excursions among the towns of Holland.

Mr. Horner resolved, therefore, to strike at once for Germany, where they were to settle down, in a measure, for the winter; he bought through tickets for Frankfort-am-Main, on a road between that town and Paris, tolerably direct, passing through a country where they would not be tempted to linger, and would not miss much during the night part of the journey. The ground is that fought over so sadly by the French, in the last war with Germany, and the stations, Saarbrück, Kaiserlauten, etc., had a melancholy sound to those of the party who remembered the daily telegraphic rumors and reports of that bitter struggle of 1870.

It was an experiment to risk this long trip; but if it were a success, it would ensure the success of the whole European excursion. It might prove that the family health could not stand it. They might all be so used up on arriving at Frankfort, that they could neither go forward, nor enjoy a rest. The family temper might not stand it. Perhaps the children would all grow so horribly cross, in their long confinement to one railway carriage, that they would be mutually unbearable. It sometimes happens. Or, if only one of the party should develop violent symptoms of selfishness, he might easily make matters so disagreeable for the rest, that they would all agree, since they could not separate, to give up in future such a trying experience.

But Mr. Horner had a good deal of faith in the nerves, tempers, and good breeding of his little band, and especially of their bodily good condition and good digestion, upon which all other qualities depend so much. Mrs. Horner was not very strong, but was cheerful, even when tired. Mary, in spite of her delicacy, showed a wonderful capacity for endurance, and her temper was so sweet, there was only danger of her allowing herself to be put upon. Bessie, solid and stolid, expected to sleep as well in her corner of the "car," as they still called it, as in her own little bed at home. Philip did not care whether he slept or not, and rather enjoyed the idea of a wakeful night. As for Tommy, they were only afraid he might get lost, in trying private excursions on his own account; but he promised all manner of obedience and propriety, and was indeed learning these virtues. Poor Miss Lejeune! She hated a night in the train, being rather fussy, as the children thought, about where and how she slept; but she fully believed in the rapid transit plan, and had advocated it from the first. It was suspected she was rather glad that Mr. Hervey was not going with them, on account of her "crinkles" in the morning, but the others were loud in their grief at parting from this dear man. Mr. Hervey, from the first, assumed that he was to be left in Paris. He was with them, however, to the last, and nodded cordially at them from the platform as the train rolled out of the station.

"How I shall miss you," he said, as he stood at the open door of their wagon, waiting the signal of departure.

"What are you going to do, now we are gone?" asked Tommy.

"Hush, Tommy!" said his mother. "Mr. Hervey never tells his plans."

Mr. Hervey laughed, saying: "My plans now are not interesting enough to tell. That business I spoke of," he added, glancing at Mr. Horner, "detains me here, I know not how long. Mind you keep me informed of your movements; and I dare say I may turn up again."

The porter shut the door, the whistle gave a little shriek, not so imposing as the long moan of an American steam-whistle, and the train was off.

"So that is the last of Mr. Hervey!" exclaimed Philip, throwing himself back in his seat with a jerk.

"Why do you say the last of him?" asked Miss Lejeune, rather sharply.

"Oh, because," replied Phil, with the air of a man of the world, "he always says he travels without a plan, so as to be free to do what he likes. I suppose now he will go and join some other party."

Mr. Horner smiled, and Mrs. Horner smiled too, but no more was said then on the subject, probably because none of them knew any-

THE POINTSMAN.

thing, and considered their guesses not worth mentioning. The young folks at the windows were soon absorbed in the scenery through which they passed.

It began to rain, and as it grew dark, nothing was to be seen but long lines of dripping landscape, varied by the stations and little houses where the pointsman lives.

"And so we have left our dear Paris!" exclaimed Mary. "I do not believe I shall like any other place as well."

"Our room at the Hotel du Rhin was so cosy," said Bessie.

"And ours," added Phil, "was splendid; you could see so much down in the place."

"And Pierre was so jolly," said Tommy. "I taught him a good deal of English."

Pierre was the garçon who brought their coffee to the salon. He was a very friendly, intelligent fellow, who had made himself useful, and they all liked him much. When they drove off from the hotel, in their small omnibus, again piled high with trunks, he stood on the sidewalk in his white apron, his hair ruffled by the parcels he had carried on his shoulder, with an expression of real regret on his face. It was their last impression of friendliness in Paris.

"Now we shall begin to talk horrid German," grumbled Bessie, "old *der-die-das* business. I know I shall not like it as well as nice easy French."

They had gone on for some time growling among themselves, lamenting their lost Paris, and making resolutions to hate the Germans and always love their Parisians, without any aid from the elders, who, tired with the getting off, were silent, until Miss Lejeune roused herself, and sitting up, said:

"Look here, children, now comes one of my sermons. I love Paris as well as you do, and think French far prettier and easier than German. But it will never do for you to go regretting along through Europe. Put your affection for Paris in your pockets, and turn your minds and hearts for what is coming next. '*Le roi est mort, vive le roi.*' Now, for the present, we have done with Louis XIV., his boulevard and all its gay shops. Who comes next to take his place?"

"Der Kaiser Wilhelm!"

"Barbarossa!"

"Charlemagne!"— exclaimed the children together, whereupon the grown-ups laughed. Mrs. Horner sighed. "I wish," she said, "the line of German monarchs was as smooth and easy as the descent of the Valois;

out it is so mixed and divided up into states that a clear idea seems difficult."

"At Frankfort we shall see the pictures of all those emperors that are in Miss Yonge's history," said Mary.

THE EMPEROR BARBAROSSA AND POPE ADRIAN.

"Must we know as much about the emperors as we do about the French kings, papa?" inquired Tommy anxiously.

"You will get very much interested in some of them," replied his father encouragingly, "and you will not be much disgraced if you do not keep the chronology of the German empire very clear. For the boundaries of Europe have been changed so often it is not easy to say what Germany is, or rather what it was, before the present emperor combined it all within one government."

"Hateful old emperor!" cried Bessie. "How I hate him for ruining the French."

"Hush! hush!" cried Miss Lejeune. "You are much too near the boundary for that!" and in fact at that moment the door was thrown open, and the guard, now become a *Schaffner*, cried, "Zwei minuten alles absteigen!" and they felt that they really had crossed the border, and entered another country.

CHAPTER XVI.

INTO GERMANY.

MARY'S letter from Frankfort to her friend and schoolmate, Cicely Stratton, will perhaps give a fair idea of first impressions in Germany.

". . We left Paris in great gloom and terror of the unknown German tongue, after our dear French, which has become quite easy to us.

MAYENCE.

The Stuyvesants, Mr. and Miss, came to see us off, — sweet of them, — with a bag full of pears and oranges. We had a good enough night on the train, though it is not exactly sleep you get with your head jammed into a corner, and each new position more uncomfortable than the last. We reached Metz at dawn, to be told that we could walk about for a few moments, then jogged on over an uninteresting country all the morning; but at two or three we began to draw near the Rhine, old castles, etc., very exciting, and the lovely sun, which we had not seen for several days, came out, with the rare phenomenon of blue sky.

"Can you not fancy us at Bingen — 'Sweet Bingen on the Rhine?'

MAYENCE CATHEDRAL.

Phil of course began to spout the poem, as if he were trying for a prize on the platform at school. Tommy's amazement at first discovering there was any sense or meaning in the lines, was good. We saw the

Maus Tower, Ehrenfells, Rudesheim, all lighted with a lovely glow; but of course we postpone any real Rhine emotions till we *do it* next spring. Then darkness came down suddenly. It was a scenic effect, there for one minute, and then gone. We had to change wagons at Mayence, and stayed there an hour. Papa and Phil walked about the town. When we got in again there was a fraülein in the same compartment, for the train was very crowded, and we tried our little German on her; and soon we reached Frankfort in the pitch dark.

"Now everybody began to be lovely and friendly, and aunt Gus to sling about her German. A sweet German in a blue blouse seized us, and we were thrust into two yellow droschkys, which are like fiacres, with one horse, but more roomy. Our driver was a lovely man, so German, who brought us at once to our hotel, where everything is clean and quiet, and where we have lots of rooms full of fluffy beds. The proprietor talks English perfectly well, which is mortifying though convenient, but we have to do German with the maids and *kellners*.

"So after a nice little dinner we sank into our first German beds, but I can't stop here to describe them, only it is like being in the middle of Charlotte Russe with white-of-egg on top.

"Baedeker has a very good plan of the town, and with it Phil. Bessie and I have been finding our way about the streets by ourselves, while papa sees bankers, and gets German money, etc. We have to come back for *table d'hôte* dinner as early as one o'clock, which seems queer after Paris. We are enchanted with Frankfort. Everything looks like Oscar Pfletsh's pictures. The streets are very muddy, and have no sidewalks, and the houses are like the underneath part of stairs. The 'Landstrasses' outside the town are rural, with trees, and very pretty, and it is all so mixed that first you are in town and then you are not, and then back again through a '*Thor*' which is no longer a Thor, but a tradition.

"In the afternoon we went, some of us, in a yellow droschky to a public garden, where we had the most lovely time. There is a big garden, and then a sort of small crystal palace, where, under glass, is a pile of artificial rock-work with water pouring over it, and palms and tree-ferns, winding paths and hidden seats. Here we wandered till the music began, and then went into the gallery of a large hall that belongs to it, and heard our first really German music. Perfectly delightful! Aunt Gus and I squeezed each other's hands at a waltz of Strauss. They go at the music with a will, and make it sound more intense than any I ever heard. Everybody, up and down-stairs, was sitting at little tables, the men smoking, women knitting, all jabbering and little minding the music. By and by we ordered tea and bread and cake. When it was all over it was dark, though still early, and we came down to the front gate to take our droschkys. Now we had a queer little adventure, because there was but one; but, as we thought there were plenty more, the others got into that and drove off, and it was mamma and I and Phil that were left. Only there were no more droschys, apparently, and two policemen kept whistling for one in vain. Suddenly one of these men (who was in a box and stuck his head out of it) cried, in German, so fiercely that we grasped his meaning, something like this: 'There's a horse-car, if you want that I'll make it stop.' 'Ja! Ja!' I said. He whistled, it stopped, and we hustled into it. Mamma was rather frightened, and asked me, as we were running to it, if I knew the way to the hotel when we got there! as if that were likely. We got into a very singular 'pferdeisenbahnwagen,' which is divided off in the middle, so that you sit with only half the passengers. This makes a sort of sociable thing of it, and all present took the wildest interest in us, and all

STATUE OF GÜTENBERG.

PALM GARDEN.

jabbered at once to tell us where to get out. A man in a peaked hat and a fraülein had a difference of opinion on this subject. The conductor came in and mixed himself in the matter, and altogether we got very merry and laughed a great deal, paid strange sums, and received little green tickets, which we have still, for it is an odd thing that in Germany they give and do not take tickets, and thus we have them all left over.

"Now we were dumped out in the middle of a dark street, with parting advice to go links and rechts. Luckily we saw the statue of Gütenburg looming up, and Phil knew how to go by that, and soon we found ourselves triumphant at our hotel, papa just paying his droschky, and looking down the street after ours, for this had all taken only a short while, luckily, so the others had not begun to worry.

FRANKFORT: LUTHER'S HOUSE.

"The chief shopping street is the Zeil, full of enchanting little shops, toys, pictures, and gay things, not pretentious, like the *magazins du boulevard* at Paris, but sort of home-like. . . ."

Frankfort, on the threshold, so to speak, of Germany, is a town full of interest historically, and very bright, pleasant, and attractive also. It dates from Charlemagne, 794. Old watch-towers in the neighborhood show the extent of the ancient city, in which the emperors were elected and crowned. An air of wealth and importance pervades the place, showing the success and extent of its commercial relations.

The Römer is, historically, the most interesting building. It was bought by the city, in 1405, for a town hall. It contains, in the "Kaisersaal," a succession of portraits of the emperors; modern pictures, it is true, and without great merit as works of art, but very useful to individualize the different heroes of the old Roman Empire, whom the children were now becoming acquainted with, as they before had learnt to know the French monarchs of importance. They spent much time among these pictures, selecting their favorites, and discussing their characters. Tommy found it hard to understand the emperors being elected, and wanted to know why in that case they were different from presidents; his father took some pains to make him see the difference between the hereditary succession of countries like France and England, where the crown descends from father to son, and the plan adopted from early times in Germany, where seven electors, acknowledged or supposed to be the wisest heads of the land, were allowed to appoint the successor of each emperor.

Three of these electors were bishops, and the others dukes or princes of large possessions and powers, and it was their business to meet and discuss and decide during the lifetime of one emperor, who should come next to him.

Mr. Horner pointed out how the two systems have not been so very different in the long run; for every emperor would naturally wish to keep the crown in his own family · and if he were strong and powerful, he could force the electors to appoint his own son or natural heir, so that it often did descend from father to son for several generations.

On the other hand, in France, where the rule was for the crown to descend from father to son, this worked very well under the same circumstances, — that is, if the king was strong and powerful; but, if he were weak and unpopular, some duke or other rival got possession of the throne and changed the dynasty, so that since the time of Charlemagne, the number of reigning families is hardly greater in the German empire than in France, where the direct succession has been lost several times, or than in England, where it has been by no means direct.

The children were beginning also to understand that in earlier times, when there was no public communication between different countries, the title of emperor, duke, or king, meant something very unlike the same words in the modern system of government. Arbitrary as the old sovereigns were, and undisputed as might be their right to control, they could not easily exercise it without railroads, telegraph, police, or newspapers. In the absence of the emperors, who often were off either alone or with whole armies, asserting their claim over the imperial city of Rome, — like Barbarossa in the picture, — making friends with the pope, or fighting as crusaders in Palestine, not only princes and nobles grew powerful, but separate cities became very strong. They had their own trades and manufactures, governed themselves, and wisely, too, by their own town-councils, training their men to arms and fortifying their walls to be a match for the nobles. Those who owned no lord but the emperor, called themselves free imperial cities. They had fleets and armies, made treaties, and were much respected; and in confused times maintained far better order than existed in other parts of the country.

Frankfort is one of these, formerly called a free town of the empire, afterwards of the German confederation. In 1866, when all Germany was united under the present emperor, all these free towns lost their individuality, and became, like any other, parts of the new Prussian empire.

The Horners saw in Frankfort the birthplace of Goethe, of whom they were destined to hear and know much more while they were in Germany, and the Ariadne, by Danneker, a beautiful piece of modern sculpture, which has been often reproduced in Parian as a statuette or mantel ornament.

CHAPTER XVII.

CHRISTMAS.

BY the advice, and through the kindness of the American Consul at Frankfort, who at that time considered it a pleasure as well as his duty, to bestow upon travellers who were his countrymen the result of his experience during a long life in Germany, Mr. Horner decided to stay there through December, and thus pass the German Christmas in that city. Mr. W——— secured for them a pleasant apartment in the Anlagen or suburbs of Frankfort, where they now settled down for these few weeks as if quite at home, even more so than at Paris; and though not venturing real housekeeping in her little establishment, as their meals were sent in from a restaurant, Mrs. Horner engaged a German maid, a stout, honest, red-faced Thuringian, named Elise, who furnished a severe test to the family German, and a source of some entertainment to the boys.

Their suite was "zweite treppe hoch," which means two flights up. The door of entrance had a bell-rope, with a handle hanging to it, exactly like the illustrations by Oscar Pfletsch. A neat little parlor connected with a smaller dining-room, and the necessary number of bedrooms; and there was a kitchen on the same floor, where Elise reigned supreme, made their coffee in the morning, washed dishes, etc. It was hard for Tommy to get used to a kitchen up-stairs, and close to the bedrooms and parlor: a funny little kitchen it was, too, with all sorts of earthen-ware pots and pans, unlike the shining tin of a Yankee pantry, but all very handy and useful.

A tall white German stove ornamented the dining-room, and became very important as the days grew shorter and the cold sharper. Happily the parlor contained a little open fire-place, so that they were not delivered over to the cheerless warmth of the national institution of Germany; but they found themselves, after all, growing attached to their ta.. .tove, although it had such a talent for going out that Elise had constantly to be summoned to kindle it again. Mary and Bessie found it very warming to lean up against, pressing their backs closely to the warm but not too hot surface, when they came in chilled through, sometimes, on a sunless day in December. In fact they had snow before they left, and Bessie had the fun of a walk in a flurry quite like a storm at home. The parlor had two windows overlooking a pretty garden, though at this season flowerless, there were window-seats, and the sashes opened like doors. Pots of pretty blossoming plants were placed in the windows by the friendly landlady, who took a great interest in her American lodgers,

GERMAN CHILDREN.

and who was a good deal surprised to find they talked English and not Indian, and that they did not eat human flesh.

In Frankfort there are many more English and Americans than in the smaller interior towns of Germany; the shops and hotels are as cosmopolitan as in other large towns; but there is a great barrier of ignorance and conservatism among the lower classes everywhere in Germany, which prevents their receiving advanced ideas. They travel not at all, read but few newspapers; an expedition of five hours on the railway is too expensive to be dreamed of; thus their notions of other nations are very primitive, and about Americans especially. They seem to think our customs are about the same now as when Columbus found them.

A GERMAN KITCHEN.

The furniture of the parlor was comfortable, but stiffly arranged, until the airy touch of Miss Lejeune had thrown a little agreeable confusion into it. Before the sofa stood the little sofa-table, where the afternoon coffee was each day brought; it was flanked on each side by a large chair, and this grouping was so dear to the heart of Elise, that whenever it was disarranged, she immediately put it all back again. This sofa is the sacred spot in a German *salon*. A seat upon it is the

BESSIE IN THE SNOW STORM.

place of honor to which the guest of most importance is conducted. Next to him or her must sit the hostess, in courteous conversation, while minor lights may cluster about them. Everything in the room was covered with some piece of worsted work or embroidery. "In fact," Mary wrote to her friend, "there is not a straight line in Germany which has not been decorated with a pattern out of the Bazar."

The carpet was stretched over the middle of the room only, while the rest of the floor, left bare, was painted and polished. Several of the other rooms had no carpets, only neatly oiled or painted floors, and a few rugs; but they were kept clean and carefully rubbed by the ever industrious Elise, who also was forever polishing bright the brass door-handles, and knobs for various uses, which abounded in the apartment.

Altogether, the Horners felt their establishment *gemüthlich*, and applied themselves, as they had in Paris, to tasting a little the characteristic life of the place. They made and received a few visits from some very pleasant German families, and thus saw something of the customs of the inhabitants; they were charmed with their simple, unpretentious manner of living, in which economy plays a conspicuous part, but where the lack of luxury is made up for by simple ornaments, worked by industrious hands—footstools, chair-tidies, coffee-warmers, everything that affection, aided by the least possible amount of money, can devise for the comfort of the home.

Now lessons began,—real serious study of the German language. Every morning, after the very simple breakfast of coffee and rolls, the dining-room was given over to grammars and dictionaries, and nothing was to be heard for some hours but the scratching of pens, and inflection of verbs, and the frequent recurrence of " der, die, das," that terrible complicated article, which now took the place of the light and airy " le " and " la " of the French. An excellent professor, Herr Saitel, recommended by Mr. W——, undertook to plant his native German in the heads of all the young Horners. He proved an admirable teacher, for he knew enough of English to understand the points of difficulty; and, unlike many German professors, did not suppose that his duties were limited to reading and explaining the principal works of Schiller and Goethe.

Even Tommy was compelled to apply himself for an hour of German reading and writing, which, in addition to what he picked up in his conferences with Elise, and all the people they met, made him a fluent, if not an accomplished German before long. There were two little German children who lived *oben*, that is, on the story above the Horners, with whom Tommy soon struck up an acquaintance. Gertrude was a solid little lass with a thick braid of blonde hair down her back, and Louis, a gentle little boy of seven.

These children were now full of the approach of Christmas, and through the whole town the preparation for that festival was apparent. Every family has a tree at Christmas as regularly as we have roast turkey on Thanksgiving Day, and, for several days beforehand, the market-place and streets were full of "Tannen-baums" leaning up against the houses, — solid little fir-trees which adapt themselves better to the candles and decorations of a Christmas-tree, than the hemlock and other growths which are found in our American woods.

The Horners were invited, through their friends, to half a dozen different trees, and, by dividing their forces, managed to see them all, thus gratifying the genuine hospitality of their friendly German acquaintances. One or two were occasions of great splendor, but the most characteristic, perhaps, was that of the little Gertrude and Louis, who lived above them, which Mary thus described in her letter to her friend : —

LOUIS.

"In a little while the tree was ready, and it was very pretty, but, except Louis and Gertrude, the others did not pretend to look at it much; for Emile and Gustel had dressed it themselves, and everybody had seen it beforehand, so there was no locking of doors and bursting in. It looked just like our trees, although Fraülein Lüdt said, 'Of course, in America you can have only imitation Tannen-baums,' thinking that the American trees all grow of pasteboard. The tree had lights and balls and candy on it, and the presents for each were set about the room on tables. The fraüleins, who were invited guests, had sweet things laid out for them. I thought they were rather rude, for though they cried 'reizend!' and 'wunderschön,' they said generally that they had got the same things

CHRISTMAS-TREE MARKET.

before. Frau Göben looked at her pile with interest. She had a black moreen petticoat and a fire-rug, and a pen-wiper, and a bottle of 'räuchend-pulver,' which they sprinkle on their stoves to partially avert a kind of burnt-iron smell inherent to their nature. That was all: but she seemed content, and so did the other relations, screaming and carrying on, just as we used to, when we looked at our presents.

"'Have you seen my pile? Look at this lovely brioche (footstool), the grandmamma made it herself.' Johanna had made and trimmed a hat for Gustel, black velvet with a rose, and Emile, who goes to Leipsic to school next week, had a trunk, and new trousers and a knife, and six pocket handkerchiefs marked in red. Everybody had a packet of pfefferkuchen. Now they brought out champagne. We all ate pfeffer-kuchen and little cakes cut out in odd shapes: cocks and hens, dogs, men, etc. The one servant came in and had her pile given her. There was to be a supper then, a great occasion, with herring-salad, made by the grandmother herself according to a time-honored custom, but we were all engaged to the W's., and came away early. The funny thing was that all this time they did not take much notice of the tree itself, which stood burning away there with its pretty little lights, and when we politely began to praise it, they said, 'Oh yes! I suppose you do not have them in America.'

"This was in English, and Tommy was so mad that he blurted out, 'Yes we do, and a hundred times better!' but I stuffed pfeffer-kuchen into his mouth, and I hope he was not heard.

"These trees were all lighted on Christmas eve, called heilig-abend. They have three feast days, the second being the real Christmas day, when everyone goes to church, and has a real Christmas dinner, and during the third the shops are still shut and the holiday continued; but the children's great time of rejoicing is Christmas eve."

CHAPTER XVIII.

MR. HERVEY.

ON the morning of Christmas, when most of the party were about to get ready for the service at the Dom-kirche, or cathedral, the postman came in rather later than usual, bearing a huge box. They had become very friendly with this postman, who was in the habit of stepping in with the letters, and having a little chat about the weather and affairs generally; on this occasion his friendship was stimulated by a Christmas-present the day before, from Mr. Horner.

All gathered about this box, much larger than anything they were accustomed to see coming by mail. The post-office service is admirable in Germany, although encumbered by certain rules and regulations which seem rather fussy to slip-shod foreigners. It takes the place of all other express business, and large packages can go by mail from one part of Germany to another in perfect safety, and very cheap.

The box was from Hamburg, and addressed to Mrs. Horner.

"It is Mr. Hervey's handwriting," shrieked Philip. Elise was summoned. Nobody knew the German for screw-driver. The Brief-träger drew from his pocket a stalwart knife, and pried off the only slightly-fastened lid, after which he disappeared in the confusion, unnoticed.

The box contained a paper box within, full of exquisite fresh-cut flowers from a green-house, marked "for the ladies," and a huge package of candies and all sorts of wonderful sugar-plums for the children. A card lay on top, inscribed:

"MUCH LOVE AND A MERRY CHRISTMAS!
FROM CLARENCE HERVEY.
HAMBURG, DEC. 23."

HAMBURG MARKET-WOMAN.

"Mr. Hervey at Hamburg!" they exclaimed; but Miss Lejeune said:—

"In all this Christmas bustle, I forgot to tell you that I had a note from him, saying he had left Paris."

"Oh, why didn't he come here!" groaned Tommy.

"But look at the beautiful things he has sent!" said Mary, and she buried her face in a delicious mass of roses, heliotropes, and all manner of perfumed blossoms.

Hamburg is celebrated for its beautiful hot-house flowers, which are not to be seen in other German towns, where it is still the fashion to make up stiff and set bouquets in regular circles, in which immortelles and evergreen predominate. Plants in pots, early bulbs, cyclamen and such things are plentiful, but the charm of cut-flowers is rare, except at Hamburg, where they are cultivated and sold in profusion.

The sugar-plums of Hamburg are also celebrated.

"And Mr. Hervey," said Philip, "is just the fellow to find that out," as he cracked a bon-bon, very delicious, between his teeth.

This pleasant reminder of their friend and countryman, gave the party the feeling of home, which the feast had otherwise lacked, and Christmas having thus happily passed, the children settled down with fresh alacrity to their German lessons, and to their study of the old emperors in the Römer, which they visited whenever they had made a new acquaintance among the **heroes of history** or tradition.

ST. HENRY.

The following is a list of the favorites among the emperors of the young Horners, with the reasons which they gave for their preference; reasons not always very deep, or perhaps to be reverenced by serious historians. Great difference of opinion prevailed among them about the characters of those they liked, and of the degree of favor that these deserved, but on the whole, so much was settled:

They liked Charlemagne (800 – 814), of course.

Otto the Great, (936 – 973), because he married Edith, sister to Athelstan of England, old friends through Freeman's Old English History.

HENRY VI.

St. Henry II., (1000 – 1024), chiefly on account of the picture of him, holding the little cathedral.

Fred'k Barbarossa, (1152 – 1178), because he is still asleep in a cave, with his long beard growing round him.

Henry VI., (1190 – 1194). for being the Cœur de Lion man, that is, the emperor who first kept Richard (his uncle, by the way) in custody and afterwards allowed his ransom, on his way home from the Crusades.

Frederick II., (1212 – 1250), was the emperor with whom Louis of Thuringia had to go off to the Crusades, leaving his wife, the saintly Elizabeth, on the Wartburg, which they were going to see in the spring.

Henry VII., (1308 – 1313), was a great Ghibelline, went to Rome to be crowned, and brought back glory to the name of German emperor. They liked his picture.

Charles IV., (1347 – 1378), was the Golden Bull Emperor.

Maximilian, (1493 – 1519), was their great favorite, on account of the Dove in the eagle's nest.

So they came to Charles V., (1529 – 1556), —

Frederick the Great, (1440 – 1796), —

But here their list became too mixed and complicated, as well as their opinions, as the number of characters increased upon a more modern stage.

They had brought with them a few books, which now proved most useful. Miss Yonge's *Young Folks' Germany*, which they had read and re-read, always interested in the stories with which she has filled it, supplemented the history of Germany in Freeman's *Historical Course*, which is less amusing, but concise and connected; they gained much light upon the subject, now that, on the very scene of their lives, the old crusaders and emperors seemed like real people, and not a confused mass of puppets. History, without any priggishness or affectation, now became a pastime with them, rather than hard work; they were always wanting to diverge from the regular route of their journeys, to some place where somebody they had read of had done something. This would have made their course a somewhat crooked journey, if all their wishes had been carried out; they had, therefore, to select, and leave much to the future.

HENRY VII.

Before leaving Frankfort, Miss Lejeune and Mary, escorted by Mr. W———, the consul, spent a day in going to Darmstadt, to see the famous Holbein Madonna, now conceded to be the real first picture of two which are so much alike that only a careful study, or comparison of their photographs, shows the differences. The other, in the gallery at Dresden where they would see it by and by, was long considered to be the original, but at the great Holbein celebration, when all his pictures were collected in Dresden, the verdict of the judges was unanimously in favor of the Darmstadt picture as the original, and most critics consider the Dresden one to be only a copy by one of Holbein's scholars, although others think it was painted later, by him.

KARL IV.

On arriving at Darmstadt, they first went to the picture gallery, and from there to the palace occupied by the Grand-duke. They were admitted by a servant in livery, to whom they said they came to see the Holbein picture. After waiting a few moments, while he went to ask admission for them, they were shown into a prettily furnished library. Crochet-work with the needle in it, just laid down, a letter on the desk, half-written, the ink not yet dry, showed that the family had but just left the room for the purpose of letting them see the picture, and would return as soon as they had left. The effect of the picture as part of the furniture of a living-room, instead of being in a stiff picture gallery, or unused palace hall, was charming; and it left a very pleasant impression on their minds of the royal family, with Holbein's lovely and benign Madonna as a constant companion during their daily life.

This picture was painted by Holbein for the burgomaster Jacob Meyer, of Basle. According to a family tradition, the youngest son of the burgomaster, who was sick, even unto death, through the intercession of the Virgin was restored to his parents; and they in grati-

JEWS' QUARTER, FRANKFORT.

tude, dedicated this offering to her. She stands on a pedestal in a richly ornamented niche; over her long, fair hair, which falls down her shoulders to her waist, she wears a superb crown; and her robe, of a dark, greenish-blue, is confined by a crimson girdle. For its purity, dignity, and peace, the face, once seen, haunts the memory. The child in her arms is generally supposed to be the infant Christ; some people have fancied that it might be intended for the little sick child recommended to her mercy. To the right of the Virgin, kneels the burgomaster Meyer with two of his sons, one of whom holds his little brother who is restored to health. On the left kneel four female figures, — of the mother, grandmother, and two daughters. All these are portraits of the real people.

MAXIMILIAN.

They noticed in the room a little paper-weight, with the words "Alice, from Victoria," which, with other little home-touches, brought more strongly to their minds than ever before, the fact that royal families are also real families, and that queens give little birthday presents and mementos to their daughters, just the same as other people do.

The princess, who used to live there, was the daughter of Queen Victoria. She married the present Duke of Hesse, who owns the picture, and they had several children; and when one of the little children had diphtheria, like any good, loving mother, she insisted upon nursing her suffering little child until it got well. But the fatigue was too much for the mother; the disease entered her system, and she herself died two days afterward. This was several years ago.

180   A FAMILY FLIGHT.

One day before they left Frankfort, Tommy, to his great delight, received a long letter from Mr. Hervey. It was from Hamburg and contained a photograph of a market-woman in the costume which is still somewhat worn there.

Mr. Hervey was charmed with the bright, clean, busy town; he described to the boys the broad streets on the Alster, which have houses on one side only, the other being open to the water, where against the solid stone embankment are boats, fastened by a ring, belonging to the families who live in these houses. It makes a lovely place to live. These sheets of water are most picturesque, and there are quantities of swans, that have been there, or their ancestors, for centuries, because a wealthy old lady made a bequest, by which they can be well taken care of.

"Think of Beacon street in Boston," wrote Mr. Hervey, "if there were no houses on the water-side, and a broad esplanade, and pleasure-boats always at hand; and if Mrs. Chevenix would leave a bequest in her will to have Charles River always full of swans!"

Mr. Hervey had been to London since they parted from him, and came over from London to Hamburg in a steamer, sailing down the Thames, and crossing the German ocean. He found it a very pretty trip, and one that they would find interesting if it came in their way. He had sailed up the Elbe to Hamburg towards night, passing the pretty little island of Heligoland before dark.

HELIGOLAND.

CHAPTER XIX.

WEIMAR.

THE Horners stayed in Frankfort until after the first of January, and then, having by this time pretty well decided what towns in Germany they most wished to visit, or rather which places they were least willing to give up, they passed the rest of the winter in going from one to another, always with some fixed object in view, whether it were a site of historic interest, a famous gallery, or even only one celebrated picture. It will not do to give a precise account of each excursion, nor to endeavor to keep the track of their time-table, their various hotels, apartments and houses in Germany. We will only pick out the plums of their pudding, and leave the rest to the guide-books. Everything relating to nature and picturesque scenery, they tried to postpone until spring; but winter travelling in Germany is not uncomfortable, and luckily the season was exceptionally mild. Their greatest discomfort was the hot, un-aired stuffiness of the railroad wagons, — the Germans having a deeply-rooted antipathy to open windows and draughts. Sometimes, when there was no nicht-rauchen-Wagen to be had, the smoke of cigars in a small compartment with all the windows shut, was quite intolerable; but the Horners, great and small, were learning the true philosophy of travel: to enjoy conveniences and not mind discomfort; and, as we have said before, good digestion, and a wise attention to sensible and regular food, supplementing, or supported by, good breeding and amiable dispositions, secured for them the power of practicing this philosophy. Everywhere they won golden opinions of their fellow-travellers, and in long trips became known as the "liebenswürdige Amerikäner," than which no praise can be found higher in the German tongue. *Liebenswürdig* is to be translated "amiable," but it means far more than our word, either from its innate force, or because the Germans attach more importance to the quality than do more emotional nations.

Without, therefore, saying exactly how they got there, or how long they stayed in each place, we will note the chief things of interest they saw in the next three months; they were looking forward, as soon as the spring opened, to a week in Eisenach, for which they were determined to wait for lovely out-door weather.

Now Miss Lejeune had once spent a whole winter in the small but celebrated town of Weimar. It was here that she had acquired her prowess in the language, and her fondness, often rebuked, for every form of sausage which is known to the German mind. It was on account of this that she was always ready to defend, and maintain with proofs, the excellence of the German cuisine, and the neatness of the German ménage;— endless discussion, always without conversion on either side, and only to be broken off by the concession,

"Well, your experience of German families must have been very different from mine."

Miss Lejeune not only longed to see Weimar once more, but to renew her affectionate intercourse with the many friends she had made there; so, while the main body of our little army passed on to Leipsic, she stopped with Mary at Weimar.

DREI GLEICHEN.

It was before they separated that, between Erfurt and Gotha they had an excellent glimpse of the Drei Gleichen castles, about which Mary roughly translated aloud this account, as they rode along, from a funny little German guide for Thüringia:—

"History mentions first the Margrave Eckbert II., of Thüringia, as their owner. As he was opposed to Henry IV., this emperor besieged his castle, in 1088, but in vain, for an attack from it forced him to a shameful retreat. Afterwards it came into the powerful family of the Counts von Gleichen, one of whom was Count Ernest, who, in 1237, took

DRESDEN: THE ZWINGER: INTERIOR VIEW.

the cross under Frederick II., but was imprisoned by the Saracens for life; but the sultan's daughter Melechsala freed him, because she loved him, and urged him to fly with her. He willingly consented, after he had convinced himself that without this step he should never regain his freedom; and, as both the Pope, and the countess, his spouse, accepted the situation, so was the double bond soon effected. The house at the foot of the berg is called the "Joy-valley," because the countess came here to meet her husband returning with his new companion, and they all three embraced each other full of joy."

"I believe that the tradition is that each wife lived in one of the castles by herself, and the count in the third," said Miss Lejeune.

"Mamma!" exclaimed Bessie, "that story is all in your Musaeus book, that we used to look at the pictures in so much, long before we knew any German. Do not you remember? I do; the very same name of Melechsala, and the pictures of Grand Cairo and Turks and Eastern things."

"I remember the book perfectly," answered her mother, *'Musaeus' Volksmärchen,* but I do not recollect that story."

"It was a long story, and you never read us the whole of it. I dare say it was stupid, but I remember the pictures. I mean to look it up when we go home, because now I can read it myself."

They had now reached the station at Weimar, about one mile from the town; here they parted.

Miss Augusta naturally felt so much at home that she did not hesitate thus to separate herself from the rest, but with Mary, who was delighted at this little escapade by themselves, she went at once to the Erb-prinzen Hotel, where she found herself still remembered.

Weimar is a more characteristic German town than Frankfort, and, indeed, than most of the large towns frequented by routine travellers.

"All the time," wrote Mary to Bessie, "while aunt Gus is being liebeüswnrdig with her Germans, I am learning my way about Weimar. By the way, it is good to have my own Baedeker! The little plan of the town is excellent, as we found at Frankfort. I must tell you about it, for you have no idea how pretty it is. From our hotel we look across the market-place to an old archway, which files of soldiers are going through constantly, and on the other side is a huge paved place, with the Schloss where the grand-duke lives, with a tall tower, and a clock that strikes hours and halves and quarters. The grand-duke's band was playing Tannhaüser while I was dressing this morning. This palace turns its back upon the town, but looks forth upon a broad and lovely park, with the Ilm running through it. It is wilder than Central Park, and full of little nooks and mossy corners. Aunt Gus and I walked there Sunday; it was a warm, spring-like day, with the frost coming out of the ground. We strayed about the paths and plucked little daisies still in bloom. not great bumping ones. like ours, but delicate English daisies.

STATUES OF GOETHE AND SCHILLER AT WEIMAR.

"This morning early aunt Gus called out to me, 'Look out of window, Mary!' and there I beheld the Platz, which has been as still as a desert before, all alive and swarming with the market, which comes twice a week. We went out and prowled about: it was so exactly like a scene

LEIPSIC: ST. NICHOLAS CHURCH.

on the stage, that when the band began to play on the balcony of the Rath-haus, we felt as if we were in an opera and must take attitudes and begin to sing. The women sat in long rows with queer things to sell, yarns and calico, real flowers and wreaths of dyed immortelles and paper roses, and fearful looking things to eat, some of them dipped up out of a barrel. Most of the women had live geese sitting by them, and there were a great many dogs.

"Last evening we went to the opera and heard the Meister Singer, delightfully played and sung and acted, and before we saw 'Ein Lustspiel.' It is the original of Mrs. Walthrop's Boarders. Aunt Gus is surprised

RATH-HAUS, LEIPSIC.

to find the town much changed and built up with new houses since she was here."

In Weimar they heard more of Goethe and Schiller, and saw the statue of the two which stands in the place before the theatre. Here also lived Wieland and Herder, and other men of literary fame, all of whom shared in the great days of Weimar, under the munificent and discriminating Grand-duke Carl August, always referred to as the Great-Grand-duke, although his present successor is a patron of music and art, keeping up the reputation of the little town for culture and æsthetic taste. The theatre is most excellent, and Miss Lejeune and Mary went often, for, as the performance begins as early as six and is often over by nine, they could do this without neglecting other invitations.

Meanwhile the others passed several days in a very good hotel at Leipsic, sight-seeing, practicing their German, and going through the Museum, where they chiefly enjoyed four beautiful landscapes by Calame, and where Mr. Horner found himself confronted by his favorite Napoleon, depicted forcibly by Delaroche in the sad moment of his fall at Fontainebleau. Mr. Horner and Philip devoted a long morning to a careful survey of the battle-field where culminated the triumph of the allied armies over their once invincible enemy.

The famous battle of Leipsic lasted four days, beginning in the morning of October 16, 1813. Until the 19th the French kept up their old renown, but in spite of all their efforts they were forced back, and at dawn on the 19th their retreat began. A large part of their army had not yet crossed the Elster when the only bridge open to them was, probably by mistake, blown up. Thousands of the French perished by drowning; and upwards of fifteen thousand were made prisoners.

A few hours afterwards the Emperor of Russia, King Frederick William of Germany, and the Emperor Francis of Austria, triumphantly entered Leipsic, and the deliverance of Germany from Napoleon was now secured.

While Philip and his father were thus engaged, Mrs. Horner indulged Bessie and Tommy in their favorite pursuit of wandering about the streets looking into shop windows, their nominal object being the headquarters of the celebrated "Tauchnitz editions" of English books. It was with some difficulty they discovered the place, and then only to find to their disappointment, as has happened to many other inquiring travellers, that the books there produced are not sold excepting to booksellers. They then went back to the very book-shop where they had received the direction for finding the Tauchnitz place, and there bought several fresh numbers of this light and agreeably printed series, greatly wondering at the intricacies of the German mind, which had deterred this salesman from saving them the trouble of a futile pilgrimage.

Leipsic is a clean and pretty town, but essentially modern, with no monuments of especial interest. The Horners thought the graceful spires of Halle, where they were left for two or three hours one day, made that a more picturesque and attractive place than the larger city.

HALLE: THE MARKET-PLACE.

CHAPTER XX.

DRESDEN.

ON an appointed day, the Horners were assembled in the large waiting-room of the modern-looking railway-station at Leipsic, and when the train was heard approaching they were allowed to come through the gates upon the platform, where they stood for a moment, bags and shawl-straps in hand, as the long row of wagons swept up and stopped. Mr. Horner and Bessie stood together, while at a little dis-

DRESDEN : BRIDGE OVER THE ELBE.

tance were Mrs. Horner with her two sons, — Philip manfully struggling with two large packages and an umbrella, Tommy almost hidden behind a huge bouquet, a parting present from the gracious landlady of their hotel.

Miss Lejeune and Mary were looking out for them from the window

DRESDEN.

of their carriage, and could hardly wait for the *Schaffner* to throw open the door.

"Here they are!" "Here we are!" all exclaimed.

"Come in here, papa!" cried Mary; "we have plenty of room. We have guarded this wagon from the people like tigers!"

And in they huddled, overjoyed to meet again after a separation of ten long days. Shawl-straps were poked up on the netting over their heads. Papa's tall hat was there relegated, while a soft cap took its place on his head.

"Well, well," said Mrs. Horner, "to think that we should meet without any mistake! I think we are born travellers."

Now all began to talk at once and to tell their experiences, more desirous of being listened to than to listen; but Miss Lejeune and Mary were fresher than the others, who had been going about all the morning for last things in Leipsic and packing: thus Mary held the floor.

"I wish you could have seen two American ladies who came from Weimar with us. We heard they had been spending the winter there, and all their friends came down to the station to meet them. Such a crowd, and such kissing and waving and cries of 'Auf wiedersehen!' I should think it was the whole German nation bidding them good-bye. One of them had a large bouquet; just like yours, Tommy, that you have there, all in stiff circles with paper round it."

"They talked German remarkably well," said Miss Lejeune. "I heard about them in Weimar; there are five of them in all, but the others stayed behind."

"Five women travelling together; just fancy!" exclaimed Mrs. Horner. "How they must quarrel!"

"I believe not," said Miss Lejeune, "though one would think so. They came out to improve themselves in languages, music, painting, and so on, and *man sagt* in Weimar they were very liebenswürdig."

"Perhaps we shall fall in with them again somewhere," remarked Mr. Horner.

"Oh, Mary!" cried Philip, "I saw Cockywax! He was in Leipsic!"

"Philip!" said his mother reprovingly. She objected to this nickname which Philip had found for the young Mr. Buffers who was with them on the steamer.

"I met him in the street," went on Philip, "and he seemed mighty glad to see me. He kept saying over and over again, 'What a delightful voyage we had; how are your sisters? Yes, that was a delightful voyage!'"

Philip gave a pretty good imitation of the embarrassed, awkward manner of the youth Buffers, which made his family laugh. Mary said: "Well, he is a nice boy, and I should like to see him again."

"I told him our hotel," continued Philip, "and I think that if you had been with us he would have called. He considers you his patron saint in the family."

"Saint Mary of Cockywax," said Bessie, adding scornfully, " I do not believe he considers me his patron saint."

"I never observed that he took any particular notice of you," retorted Philip.

"Come, come, children, do not quarrel," said the mamma. Bessie and Philip, or Jack, as they called him half the time, were excellent friends, but so near in age that they sometimes roughed each other.

Soon they were approaching Dresden, as so often they had before drawn near large cities, in the glowing western light. The flowing river, with its ample bridges, makes a beautiful town of it, as well as the handsome buildings with which it is plentifully provided.

In Dresden they remained some time, for there was much to see. They were established in one of the large hotels in the middle of the town, and for the first time joined the table d'hote dinner, instead of being supplied, as in Paris, in their own rooms. They found, for a change, some amusement in the variety of characters they thus met. The table held no more than twenty guests of different nationalities, among whom German was the least represented. In fact, the Horners congratulated themselves that they had secured some familiarity with German at the other towns they had visited, before coming to Dresden; for it is so over-run with English and Americans that, even in the *pensions*, their language is as much spoken as the native one. In the shops and streets English is constantly

MADONNA DE SAN SISTO.

ENAMEL FRAME IN THE GREEN VAULT.

heard; and, except that, from preference, they all, except **Mrs. Horner**, chose to exercise their skill in talking German, they could have done perfectly well without a knowledge of it.

There was a party of second-rate English at their table, whose chief occupation consisted in staring, especially at the Horners. Very likely this was the first time they had seen civilized Americans, and that they were on the look-out for some traces of Indian manners and customs. As the Horners were perfectly well trained in the use of the knife and fork and other modern utensils, the starers found very little to gratify them; but once Phil heard one of the daughters say out quite loud to another, "She has eaten her push-piece!" Phil turned round to look at Bessie, on whom the four eyes had been glued. She was just finishing her fish, and had ended, very improperly, by putting the piece of bread in her mouth which she had been using. This was ever after called the "push-piece" by the Horners; and these people went by the title of the Push-pieces, whenever they were referred to; but they never saw them again, for they left the very next day.

The Grosse-Garten was already attractive on some of the spring days in the end of February. The Green Vault amazed some of them with a mass of jewelry, mosaic, crowns, and other splendors; but the Zwinger, on account of the celebrated picture-gallery it contains, was the place to which they devoted the most time, and where Mary and Miss Lejeune continued their study of the old masters.

Naturally the first picture they sought was the other Holbein Madonna; and Mary thought she could remember that the Darmstadt one was superior in execution and intention; but so much might be due to having seen that first, she was willing to allow that her judgment was not worth much.

Mrs. Horner took intense pleasure in the renowned Madonna di San Sisto, by Raphael. It had been, through engraving and photograph, her favorite picture for years. She was willing to sit before the large picture, lending herself to a kind of dream as she gazed upon it, thus rather irritating the more fastidious judgment of Miss Lejeune, who no longer concedes the first place among artists to Raphael.

Miss Lejeune, however, was capable of deviating from the narrow paths of the Pre-Raphaelites, for she confessed to considering the

DRESDEN ENTRANCE TO THE ZWINGER, AND THE STATUE OF FREDERICK AUGUSTUS.

Magdalen of Battoni, also in the Dresden gallery, one of the most beautiful pictures in the world; and this is decidedly modern.

In this gallery Mary renewed her search for the masters of the old schools. She lingered over the oldest pictures, seeking to learn in what their charm consisted, and rejoiced to find that she really could like them, and that affectation would consist in calling them "horrid old things," which many young Americans feel called upon to do to avoid the very imputation.

It was very odd to the Horners to come in Saxony upon a royal family and royal state, playing at king and queen in a baby-house, as Bessie called it. Although, as they remembered, by the union of Germany, Kaiser William was declared emperor of the whole of it, in the Hall of Mirrors at Versailles, in 1871, the kings, grand-dukes, and dukes of the uniting parts retain all their titles and their ancient rights, something like the separate government of our States under the President; thus, at Weimar, the grand-duke holds his own court, and receives an ambassador from the imperial court at Berlin. At Dresden they often saw the royal family and the king and queen of Saxony driving out in state. The royal family of Saxony are Catholics; and Passion Week, which took place while the Horners were in Dresden, was observed with much solemnity. The shops were closed, the churches were open; the services were very impressive, even to children of Puritan descent. On Easter Sunday, especially, the cathedral ceremony was long and solemn, but to their minds, in spite of the fine music, tedious.

But all Germany defers to the glory of the Emperor William, and the Horners heard so much of the beloved Kaiser that they longed for Berlin, where he was to be seen in all his splendor.

"But," said Bessie, "he is only a *parvenu* kind of emperor. I do not consider him a descendant of our Barbarossa at all. I think the Austrian emperors are more like that."

"True," said her father, "but you must remember that Francis II. formally resigned the imperial crown, in 1806."

"Because your favorite Napoleon frightened him to death," resumed Bessie. "I consider that to be the real end of German history, just like the end of a novel; and this empire, which the Kaiser has started, is not so old a nation as the United States."

"Do not say that in Berlin, or, if you do, do not use your best German, or you may be arrested for seditious sentiments," said Mr. Horner good-humoredly.

Spring was really come, and in the first tender days, when everything is pink and yellow, and soft vague green, before the leaves have hidden the grace of the branches, the Horners spent a week in "Saxon Switzerland," which is the name the country goes by about Dresden. They stayed at a pleasant little inn at Schandau, close upon the river Elbe, and from here made excursions, as the weather allowed, chiefly on foot, to the points of interest about them.

This return to out-door life and to the attractions of nature, was pleasing to all of them. They rejoiced greatly when the first of May approached, and they broke up camp in Dresden for a few weeks in beautiful Eisenach. "I declare," exclaimed Bessie, "I wish never to see a church or a picture-gallery again. I want woods and castles and cataracts."

"And no dates and dynasties," added Tommy.

SAXON SWITZERLAND: THE PREBISCHTHOR. A COLOSSAL NATURAL ARCH.

CHAPTER XXI.

SAINT ELIZABETH.

IN the year 1207, Andreas II. was king of Hungary, and Hermann, the patron of the Minnesingers, was landgrave of Thüringia, and held his court in the castle of the Wartburg.

In that year, the queen of Hungary had a daughter, whose birth was announced by many blessings to her country and kindred; for the wars which had distracted Hungary ceased, and peace and good-will reigned, at least for a time; the harvests had never been so abundant: crime, injustice, and violence had never been so infrequent as in that fortunate year. Even in her cradle, Elizabeth showed that she was the favorite of heaven. She was never known to weep from crossness, and the first words she distinctly uttered, were those of prayer; at three years old, she was known to give away her toys and take off her rich dresses to bestow them on the poor; and all the land rejoiced in her early wisdom, goodness, and radiant beauty.

These things being told to Hermann of Thüringia, he was filled with wonder, and exclaimed:

"Would to God that this fair child might become the wife of my son!" and thereupon he sent an embassy to the king of Hungary, to ask the young princess in marriage for his son, Prince Louis, bearing rich presents. His messengers were hospitably received, and returned to the Wartburg with the little princess, who was then four years old. The king, her father, bestowed on her a cradle and a bath, each of fine silver, and of wondrous workmanship; and silken robes, curiously embroidered with gold, and twelve noble maidens to attend upon her.

When the Princess Elizabeth arrived at the castle of the Wartburg, at Eisenach, she was received with infinite rejoicings, and the next day she was solemnly betrothed to the young Prince Louis; and the two children being laid in the same cradle, they smiled and stretched out their little arms to each other, which thing pleased the Landgrave Hermann and his wife Sophia, and all the ladies, knights, and minstrels who were present regarded it as an omen of a blessed and happy marriage.

DIE WARTBURG BEI EISENACH.

From this time the children were not separated; they grew up together, and every day they loved each other more and more.

Louis soon perceived that his Elizabeth was quite unlike all the other children in the court; all her infant thoughts seemed centred on heavenly things; her very sports were heavenly, as though the angels were her playmates; but charity and compassion for the suffering poor, formed, so to speak, the staple of her life. Everything that was given to her she gave away, and she collected what remained from the table, and saved from her own repasts every scrap of food, which she carried in a basket to the poor children of Eisenach.

As long as the Landgrave Hermann was alive, no one dared to oppose the young Elizabeth in these exercises of devotion and charity, but he died when she was about nine years old, and Louis sixteen, and Elizabeth having thus lost in him a father and protector, became a forlorn stranger in her adopted home; for the Landgravine Sophia disliked her, her future sister, the Princess Agnes openly derided her, and the other ladies of the court treated her with great neglect. Meantime, Louis, her betrothed, was watching her closely. He did

THE WARTBURG: CASTLE COURT.

not openly show her any attention, and had some doubts whether she were not too far above him in her austere, though gentle piety. But often when she suffered from the unkindness of others he would secretly comfort her, and dry up her tears. And when he returned home after an absence, he would bring her some little gift, either a rosary of coral, or a little silver crucifix, a chain, or a golden pin, or a purse, or a knife; and when she ran out to meet him joyfully, he would take her in his arms and kiss her right heartily.

It happened on one occasion, that Louis went on a long hunting excursion with some neighboring princes, and was so busy with his guests, that when he returned he brought her no gift, nor did he salute her as usual. Those courtiers who were the enemies of Elizabeth, marked this well; she saw their cruel joy, and in the bitterness of her grief, she confided it to her old friend Walther, who had brought her, an infant, from Hungary, who had often nursed her in his arms, and who loved her as his own child. A few days afterward, this Walther, as he attended the landgrave to the chase, asked him what were his intentions with regard to the Lady Elizabeth:

"For," said he, "it is thought by many that you love her not, and that you will send her back to her father."

On hearing these words, Louis, who had been lying on the ground to rest, started to his feet, and throwing his hand toward the lofty Inselberg which rose before them, exclaimed:

"Seest thou yon high mountain? If it were all of pure gold from the base to the summit, and if it were offered to me in exchange for my Elizabeth, I would not give her for it. No; I love her only, and I will have my Elizabeth!" Then from the purse which hung at his belt, he drew forth a little silver mirror, curiously wrought, surmounted with an image of the Saviour. "Give her this," he added, "as a pledge of my troth."

Walther hastened to seek Elizabeth with the gift and loving message. She smiled an angel smile and kissed the mirror, reverently saluting the image of Christ. About a year afterward their marriage was solemnized with great feasts and rejoicings which lasted three days.

Louis was at this time in his twentieth year. He was tall, with fair hair and blue eyes, and a noble brow. He was of a princely temper, resolute, yet somewhat bashful; and he was faithful to his Elizabeth to the hour of his death.

Elizabeth was not quite fifteen. Her beauty, though still immature, was that of her race and country; a tall, slender figure, a clear brown complexion, large, dark eyes, and hair black as night; her eyes glowed with an inward light of love and charity, and were often moistened with tears.

She loved her husband tenderly, but she carried into her married life the austere piety which had distinguished her from her infancy; she rose in the night to pray, kneeling on the bare ground; she wore hair-cloth next her tender skin, and would scourge herself, and cause her ladies to scourge her. Louis sometimes remonstrated, but he secretly thought that he and his people were to benefit by the sanctity of his wife. She was always cheerful and loving to him, dressed to please him and often rode to the chase with him. When he was away, she put on the dress of a widow till his return, when she would again array herself in her royal mantle, and meet him with a joyous smile.

The most famous story about her is that one day, in the absence of her husband, during a severe winter, she left her castle with a single attendant, carrying in the skirts of her robe a supply of meat, bread, and eggs to a poor family; and as she was descending the frozen and slippery path, her husband, returning from the chase, met her bending under the weight of her charitable burden.

"What dost thou here, my Elizabeth?" he said; "let us see what thou art carrying away," and she, confused and blushing to be so discovered, pressed her mantle to her bosom, but he insisted, and opening her robe, he beheld only red and white roses, more beautiful and fragrant than any that grow on this earth, even at summer-tide, and it was now the depth of winter! Then he was about to embrace his wife, but looking in her face, he was overawed by a supernatural glory which seemed to emanate from every feature, and he dared not touch her; he bade her go on her way and fulfill her mission.

SAINT ELIZABETH.

In the year 1226, the landgrave Louis accompanied his lord, the emperor Frederick II., into Italy. In the same year a terrible famine afflicted all Germany, and Thüringia suffered most of all. Elizabeth distributed to the poor all the corn in the royal granaries. Every day a certain quantity of bread was baked, and she herself served it out to the people, who thronged around the gates of the castle, sometimes to the number of nine hundred; uniting prudence with charity, she so arranged that each person had his just share, and so husbanded her resources that they lasted through the summer; when harvest time came round, she sent all the people to the fields provided with scythes and sickles, and to every man she gave a shirt and a pair of shoes. When the plague followed the famine, she founded two hospitals in Eisenach; went herself from one to the other, ministering to the inmates with a cheerful countenance.

THE PARTING.

In the following year, all Europe was armed for the third crusade; and Louis must join the banner of his emperor. He took the cross, with many other princes and nobles at Hildesheim; but on his way thence to Wartburg, he took off his cross and put it into his purse, till he should have prepared his wife for the pain of parting, — but many days passed away, and he had not courage to tell her. One evening, she playfully unbuckled his purse, seeking alms for her poor; she drew forth the cross. Too well she knew the sign; the truth burst upon her, and she swooned at his feet.

They parted with tears. The landgrave pursued his journey toward Palestine, but at Otranto he was seized with a fever and died. He commanded his knights and counts to carry his body home, and to defend his Elizabeth and his children with their life-blood, if need were, from all wrong and oppression.

But now the eldest brother of Louis, Henry, wickedly took possession of his lands, and banished the widow and children from the Wartburg.

It was winter-time, and the snow lay upon the ground, when this daughter of kings was seen slowly descending the rough path, carrying a new-born baby in her arms; her women followed with the three children. Henry had forbidden any one to harbor her, resolved to drive her away from his territory; so she wandered about with her children till she at last found refuge in a poor inn; and afterward supported herself by spinning wool.

When the knights returned to Thüringia, bearing the remains of Louis, they were filled with indignation at what had happened. They obliged Henry to be contented with the title of regent only, gave young Hermann, the son of Louis and Elizabeth, his father's place, and endowed Elizabeth with the city of Marbourg, whither she retired with her daughters.

And here she might have ended her days tranquilly, but for the severe tyranny of the priest Conrad, her confessor, who made of her life one long penance. Finally he dismissed even her two women, who had served her faithfully. She was said to be surrounded by celestial visitants; that the blessed Virgin herself deigned to converse with her, and she gradually faded away, till, laid upon her last bed, she turned her face to the wall and began to sing hymns with a most sweet voice. When her strength failed, she uttered the word "silence," and so died. She had just completed her twenty-fourth year, and had survived her husband just three years and a half.

No sooner had Elizabeth breathed her last breath than the people surrounded the couch, tore away her robe and cut off her hair for relics. Four years after her death she was canonized as a saint, by the Pope; and her shrine, in the church of Saint Elizabeth, at Marbourg, has been venerated and visited ever since.

FRIEDRICH II. PUTTING ON THE CROWN OF JERUSALEM.

CHAPTER XXII.

EISENACH.

SUCH is the charming story of the holy Elizabeth, told by Miss Lejeune as they came towards Eisenach, about the middle of May. The spring was fairly open, the weather had begun to be mild and lovely; the landscape through which the Horners were passing was deliciously fresh with delicate green tints. All promised them a delightful country week.

The station was reached. The family climbed into droschkys, the baggage followed, and they rumbled along over the rough stone

"THE STORKS ARE HERE!" CRIED TOMMY.

pavement, under the old arch of the Nicholas Gate, and found themselves in the quaintest and most picturesque German town they had yet seen. Their hotel was on one side of a sort of square which was all up-hill; the red-tiled and gabled roof of each house made a step up from its lower neighbor; the houses were painted different colors, and gaily-striped awnings increased the variety of tint. Behind and above all, exactly like the backscene at the theatre, rose the Wartburg, with the pretty castle on its summit, near and yet far, for while it seemed to overhang them, it still looked small with distance. When they arrived, it was toward evening, and the castle glowed with pink light and violet shadows. It was an ideal castle, just fit for the home of Saint Elizabeth. Every Horner, old and young, was full of rejoicing. They had a good German supper, and went to bed, in their funny German beds, with their heads full of anticipation. The clock in the market-square hard by, struck the hours and the quarter hours as they were falling off to sleep. They felt as if they had been put back by magic into the thirteenth century, or thereabouts.

THE ANNATHAL AT EISENACH.

The next day the weather did not disappoint them; and they started early to make the ascent of the mountain, Mrs. Horner and Miss Lejeune mounted on mild donkeys with long ears and wise faces, the rest on foot, with stout sticks to rest on.

A short walk through the town brought them to the actual ascent, of less than quarter of a mile, on a well-made path. It is steep, but winding, and not more fatiguing than the many steps to views on the top of towers, to which the younger Horners had now become accustomed. Tommy, of course, started at a rapid pace, and distanced them all; they soon found him sitting on a stone, with a red face, and out of breath, after which he kept nearer the party. This was a straggling one; the donkeys, who had no great enthusiasm about reaching the top, were inclined to take it easy; and Mr. Horner was equally in favor of a leisurely pace.

"Look at that party of Germans, Philip," he said. "They put a system into it. They do a certain distance, and then they stand still and breathe a few moments, before starting again."

"Yes, but papa," replied Jack, "one would think we were ascending Popocatapetl, to make such a time of it!" and he started off on a spurt.

In fact it is but a trifling climb, a little over six hundred feet, and the views from the mountain side are so pretty as to afford a good excuse for resting pauses.

The Wartburg was built in 1067. In the eight centuries which have passed over it since much of it had gone to ruin; but the present grand-duke of Saxe-Weimar has restored the castle as nearly as possible to its original state; so that, while its foundations are very ancient, the decorations are excessively modern, but executed in a spirit so faithful to tradition that it is like looking at a bran-new piece of antiquity.

The life of Saint Elizabeth is illustrated by a series of modern frescoes; and the lives of various landgraves are made the subject of another series, of which the favorite of the Horners explains the name of the castle:

> Landgrave Louis the Springer came one day while he was chasing a stag, to the top of this mount; astonished at the lovely view, the thought arose in him here to build a castle, and he is said to have exclaimed,
> "Wart, Berg, du sollst eine Burg werden!" — "Wait, mount, thou art to be a castle."
> The tradition says that the name Wartburg originated from these words.

ISABELLE OF PORTUGAL, WIFE OF CHARLES V.

EISENACH. 219

The Wartburg is the place where Luther found protection after the Diet of Worms. When Charles V. was elected emperor, Luther and his party hoped he would declare himself in favor of their views for reforming the Church. The Papal Legate, on the other hand, wanted the emperor to take measures against Luther at once. When he held his first diet, or assembly, at Worms, he sent for Luther, and tried to make him retract his heresies, so called; but Luther would not. He allowed him to go away in safety, but immediately issued an edict condemning him as a heretic. So Frederick of Saxony, who was a friend of Luther, had him waylaid and seized, like a prisoner, and carried to the Wartburg; but it was really to get him out of the way of his enemies. He stayed there almost a year, and it was there he wrote his translation of the New Testament. His room is shown, very little changed. The ink-spot on the wall has been painted out, where it was said he threw his inkstand at the devil. Perhaps it was only a fly that came and bothered him.

CHARLES V.

The Horners spent a long day upon the Wart *Berg*, examining the *Burg*, enjoying the lovely views from the windows, and the still remaining portions of the ancient castle as much as the modern pictures, and the legends of the guide. They found a very good lunch at the restaurant on the mountain, and came back to their hotel, tired but happy, for a good dinner.

Mary and Philip went up there the very next day, on foot, and Mary took her sketching things. She was not very skillful, but very persevering, and her modest little book was gradually getting filled with many a sketch which she enjoyed afterwards, as recalling not only the place, but the mood, in which it was made.

On this second day, Mrs. Horner rested, while the others wrote letters, made short sallies into the town, and enjoyed the band in the market-place at noon, when all the inhabitants of Eisenach turned out and strolled about.

One day was spent in wandering about the paths and climbing the rocks in the Anna-thal. They took a little boy for a guide, who carried an ample basket of lunch, so they need not come back till late. The Anna-thal is a narrow ravine; the wildest part of it is called the Drachen-schlucht, and here the steep sides are covered with moss and ferns, and wet with trickling moisture. It was a very warm day, so that the damp and coolness were most agreeable; though Mrs. Horner mentioned the word "rheumatism," she was immediately suppressed.

The Anna-tha. is not on a grand, imposing scale; it is simply very, very pretty, and something like the ravines in the White Mountains. The paths have been cared for and cleared of underbrush, but not too much "fixed up." On a huge rock at the end of an opening is to be seen a large dark letter A, marked upon the stone in honor of a visit to the spot by Anna, queen of Holland, the mother of the late grand-duchess of Weimar.

There are similar letters like this A in famous picturesque places through Germany, put up to commemorate the presence of great personages. They mar the landscape less than the sprawling advertisements, such as "Break of Day Bitters," which disgrace the scenery in America; and their intention at least is more æsthetic and in harmony with nature.

The Horners had what we call "a real nice time," at Eisenach. They settled down as it was their custom, and each one went upon his way, according to his own sweet will. Their German was good enough now to serve. Tommy made friends with the excellent landlady, and became initiated in the plucking of chickens and skinning of hares.

They went to the old church, and enjoyed the simple service,

EISENACH. 221

and the serious faces of the congregation. The service in the churches of Germany, even where it is Catholic, seems more earnest and more Protestant than that of the cathedrals of Southern Europe. Protestantism matches both the climate and the turn of

LUTHER IN THE CELL.

thought of the German people. It is as if Luther had left his stamp in the very shrines where the reformed religion is not acknowledged.

Charming weather, pleasant drives, and simple, quiet life made their visit to Eisenach a memorable one. The children found traces here, as elsewhere, of their favorite, or detested kings and emperors, and in connection with Luther, learned more of Charles V., and his wife Isabelle.

There is a palace at Eisenach interesting as the home, for a long time, of the duchess of Orleans, the wife of that duke of Orleans who was killed by a fall from his carriage in 1842. He was the son of Louis Philippe, then reigning, so that he was his heir to the throne, and by his death his son became the heir apparent. His widow, the mother, was a German princess. She devoted herself to the education of the young prince, and, after the abdication of Louis Philippe, she came to Eisenach, accepting an invitation of the grand-duke of Weimar, who was her uncle. Here she lived, honorably fulfilling her duties as a mother and a Christian, and maintaining the claims of her son, whom she long cherished the hope of seeing on the throne of France. When she saw his prospects blasted by the success of Louis Napoleon, disappointment preyed upon her mind, her health failed, and she died while on a visit to England, in 1858.

Her story is a sad one, and led the young Horners to revert once more to the eventful ups and downs of the princes of France. This son of hers was called Louis Philippe Robert, Comte de Paris, and heir to the throne of the Bourbon family.

CHAPTER XXIII.

A BOMB.

"BERLIN, MAY 10th, 1881.

"*My Dear Mr. Horner:* — What are your plans? Perhaps you have not any. What do you say to Norway? I think I shall start for the midnight sun and way-stations, about the first of June, and I need not say that it will be far pleasanter for me if you decide to join me with your party. A month is enough to devote to Norway, and I think Mrs. Horner and the young ladies would enjoy the trip. Let me hear from you at once.

"Truly yours, CLARENCE HERVEY."

THIS letter burst like a bomb at the Horners' breakfast-table, one day at Eisenach. They had no more thought of going to Norway than they had of going to Japan; and the midnight sun had entered into their plans as little as the pyramids at Cairo.

"How exactly like Hervey!" exclaimed Mr. Horner irritably. The idea disturbed the tenor of his thoughts somewhat roughly. Their month at Eisenach had been very pleasant. The fields were full of wild flowers, and every day the children came in with their hands full. It was a healthy sort of out-door life that they did not like to think of leaving; and yet the time was coming when they must move on. Their rooms were already engaged at Berlin, and for some time the wise heads of the party had been thinking about their future course, consulting guide-books and maps, in order to lay out the plan for their summer months; but the children had but little part in the practical discussion of such things.

Mr. Horner had some affairs to attend to in Antwerp, sooner or later; one plan had been to spend the month of June in Holland. Norway was a wholly new suggestion.

"Mr. Hervey was always talking about Norway on the voyage," said Mary, "do not you remember?"

"I think he meant to go to Norway when he left America," said Miss Lejeune, "only he never makes plans. He told me that he hoped to go some time; and he had all kinds of Norway Murray's and other guides with him, that a friend of his handed over to him who had made the trip."

WILD FLOWERS.

"How I should like to go!" exclaimed Mary. "I always wanted to see the midnight sun."

"I do not care half so much for Norway as for European cities," declared Philip.

"Do not you?" replied Mary. "Oh, I do! and then we have seen so many cities."

"I wonder what it is like," exclaimed Bessie. "Let's get the Baedeker and see."

"But we have no guide-book that will tell," said Mary. "'Northern Germany' says nothing about Norway."

"Think of seeing real Norsemen and vikings!" exclaimed Bessie; "I hope we shall go!"

"Rubbish," replied Phil, "the vikings are all dead, and there are nothing but stupid Swedes and Norwegians, like that Emma we had, who could not speak any English."

While the children were thus chattering without any responsibil-

MIDNIGHT SUN.

ity, the three older people remained silent, but each was busily thinking, and weighing the subject internally.

It was after the young ones had scattered to their out-of-doors pursuits that a grave consultation was held. Miss Lejeune took out her interminable knitting, Mr. Horner lighted his cigar, and Mrs. Horner, wrapping a light shawl about her shoulders, leaned back in an American chair, as they call a rocking-chair in Europe, and rocked gently as they talked.

"Well, what do we think of this Norway plan?" demanded Mr. Horner.

More than one council was needed before any decision was reached; and several letters were exchanged with Mr. Hervey; the verdict was that they had better come to Berlin, and talk it over with him. This occasioned no change in their plan, for it was quite time for them to leave Eisenach. The only difference was that now their quiet life was broken up, and they no longer cared for their country pursuits. When the time for leaving a place has come, there is an end to the enjoyment of it. Unsettled feelings take the place of satisfaction. The last few days in a place are always uncomfortable; as Phil expressed it, "The bottom has come out, and there is no more fun."

Besides, they were all in a hurry to see their dear Mr. Hervey again; and Tommy was longing to behold the emperor of Germany in all his glory. They bade good-bye to Eisenach friends, especially to a little family of children and dolls, with whom Bessie and Tommy had become very intimate.

So to Berlin they went, and to the hotel where Mr. Hervey had his room. He came to wait for them at the station, and the meeting was a very joyous one.

They had a merry and rather noisy dinner the first evening, for every Horner wished to tell Mr. Hervey, in his or her own way, everything which had happened to them since they left him in Paris. It was the children's occasion; for the parents thought it was hopeless to try to get a word in edgewise, and so they allowed the young tongues to run freely; only Mrs. Horner faintly murmured once or twice.

"Not quite so loud, Tommy."

The end of many conferences was, as it was very apt to be, that Mrs. Horner had her own way. She was so quiet and gentle that an outside observer would not suppose that she was the general in command of the party; but her ideas were always so excellent that her husband invariably surrendered to them, and so did Miss Lejeune, although in the present case she demurred at first.

Mrs. Horner's plan was to divide the party! When she first proffered it the others looked

BESSIE'S PLAYMATES.

aghast; but her reasons were ready. She thought there were altogether too many for Norway, "where," she said, "I believe you have to ride in little carriages all by yourself. It will not do to have a long string of Horners all across the country, from the North Cape to Copenhagen." She told her husband privately that she thought the burden of the party would rest too heavily on Mr. Hervey, who would be the natural guide, as he had studied up the subject. Mr. Horner assented to this. Indeed, his chief objection to the plan was, that it imposed such an army on Mr. Hervey.

"Yes," continued Mrs. Horner, "this is really the best plan. If you, Augusta, will chaperon the party that

NORWEGIAN CARRIAGE.

goes, I think I will not go myself, but will form a camp somewhere with the rest of the children. We shall be perfectly comfortable and happy, and indeed I shall like it much better than so much sea-travel. I will keep Tommy; and, Mr. Hervey, you may choose, of the others, which you will take."

Mr. Hervey did not exactly choose; but different reasons now settled the division of the forces. Mr. Horner stayed with his wife, and, strange to say, Philip preferred to be left behind. There was something manly in this; he did not like to desert his mother; besides, he did not care so much for scenery as for things and people. Both the girls might as well go, as they could share the same room.

As for Tommy, no one dared to break to him the news that he was to remain behind; and finally Mr. Hervey begged so hard to take him that Mrs. Horner yielded, and Tommy never knew that the first plan had not included him. Mrs. Horner was reluctant; but Mr. Hervey came and sat by her, and took her hand, saying, "Now, Mrs. Horner, you know that you keep Tommy because you think that he will be a torment to me. Look me in the eyes, and say, honestly, that this is the case."

Mrs. Horner laughed, blushed, looked up and said, "That is the case!"

"Very well. Now hear me solemnly affirm and assert that I want him to go with us to Norway."

And so it was settled that Tommy should go.

Miss Lejeune, who usually made all their plans, had singularly little to say about this one. She assented very readily to the charge of the girls, but declared herself willing to be left behind, if that were considered best. Of course this was not thought of for an instant; and, when it was decided, she lent herself to the scheme with her usual alacrity.

After these tedious discussions were over and the thing was settled, the Horners applied themselves to sight-seeing in Berlin, for while they were still uncertain what was to happen to them, they had done little else than speculate upon the future.

Mrs. Horner may have been secretly a little sad, to find her brave proposal for a division so successful; but she said nothing of this, and averred that the month of separation would be short. Mr. Horner was relieved of the responsibility of engineering his family through a difficult region; and he found, moreover, that his presence in Antwerp was really important, on account of the affairs of his firm.

Bessie was sorry to part with Jack, but consoled herself with thinking she could write to him, and hear from him.

"It will be the same," she added, "as if we all went to both places at once, for we can tell each other all about them."

They packed industriously, for, as usual, all their possessions were scattered, far and wide, about their rooms at the hotel. It was now necessary to exercise more than ordinary thought about their luggage, because in Norway it is best to be as lightly burdened as possible. The smallest trunks were now emptied and put at the disposition of the Norwegians. A double valise sufficed for both Bessie and Mary. Miss Lejeune's ample trunk was replaced by a modest hat-

MONUMENT OF VICTORY, BERLIN.

box; and Tommy's things were destined for a corner of Mr. Hervey's portmanteau. It was really very good-natured of this gentleman to assume the care of the boy; but he was wholly in earnest about it. This modest array of boxes was supplemented by manifold wraps in shawl-straps.

CHAPTER XXIV.

BERLIN.

THE capital of Germany is a handsome city, and the Germans are justly proud of it, and "Unter den Linden" is a distinguished avenue, although the lime-trees which give it this odd and pretty name, are not the noblest specimens of their kind. It is remarkable for its width, and for the fine buildings and gay shops with which it is lined.

Berlin is comparatively modern; it owes its existence, as a city of importance, to the uncle of Frederick the Great, who, having created a kingdom, required a capital for it. The great Frederick, whose passion, like that of Louis XIV., was for building and architecture, adorned it with new buildings, and enriched it with works of art. The present emperor has the ambition, shared by all the Germans, to make Berlin the finest city in the world.

It lacks, however, the antiquity of Paris, and with it, much of the charm of historical association.

The Horners were in Berlin ten days or a fortnight, and at a lovely season of the year, but unfortunately, their usual good luck in weather deserted them. It rained continuously, almost all the time, with that perseverance which the heavens sometimes show even in leafy June. All the excursions they took had to be in closed droschkys or under umbrellas, and the only day the sun was out they had devoted to the pictures in the Berlin Museum, thinking it was sure to rain again that day.

The Norway plan, moreover, with the consequent division of the party it entailed, unsettled all their minds, and gave to each one the vague feeling of unrest, which sometimes takes possession of the traveller,

PALACE OF THE CROWN PRINCE.

and deprives him, while it lasts, of the power to enter into the present scene, and grasp the meaning of the objects of interest under his notice. Every one who has travelled, remembers places which failed, for reasons of this sort, to make their due impression. The Horners said afterward that they did not like Berlin; if they had been there

QUEEN LOUISE AND NAPOLEON.

under other circumstances, they would have found it, as have many enthusiastic visitors, a delightful place.

Nevertheless, they succeeded in seeing, between the drops, the chief buildings of importance. They drove to Charlottenburg, to see the mausoleum which holds the beautiful marble monuments of Frederick William III. and his wife, the parents of the present emperor.

It was prince William III. who had to bear the brunt, in his kingdom, of Napoleon's ambition, who, jealous of the independence of Prussia, was determined to humble it. The battle of Jena was the consequence, and Bonaparte entered Berlin as a conqueror. The queen Louise, beautiful and popular, sought to mediate with Napoleon, but he treated her with great rudeness. He carried off with him the sword of

BRANDENBURG GATE.

Frederick the Great, and the Car of Victory from the Brandenburg gate.

These things heaped up bitterness between the French and Germans. The crowning of the present emperor at Versailles, in 1871, was the *revanche* of the Germans.

As the Horners drove under the Brandenburg gate, Mr. Horner pointed out this chariot, with its four bronze horses, saying:

"They have travelled farther than steeds of their material are

ZOOLOGICAL GARDEN.

apt to; having made the journey to Paris and back again." For after Napoleon's abdication, the bronze horses were restored.

Mary and Miss Lejeune were the ones who enjoyed Berlin the most. They were often missing from the party of sight-seers, and if so, only to be found before their beloved old masters, catalogue in hand. The picture-gallery of the Berlin Museum, though inferior to to those of Dresden and Munich, contains good pictures by a greater number of different masters, especially of the old German and Italian schools, and is admirably adapted for the study of the history of art, as the rooms are arranged in order, according to the different schools. In each apartment, a list of the pictures it contains is hung on the wall.

Mr. Hervey took Bessie and the boys to the Zoölogical Garden, where they saw delightful beasts; but the *Nil-Pferd* (Nile-horse) or hippopotamus, which used to be there, is dead.

The theatre and opera at Berlin are admirable. They saw *Don Carlos*, Schiller's play, finely performed; and were delighted to find that their knowledge of German was so much improved that they understood very well, although not every word.

Meanwhile, in the evenings not otherwise employed, and also in the rainy mornings, they were busy reading up about Norway, while Mr. Hervey was getting together his guide-books and picking up information wherever he could, about travelling in that country. They had conversation-books in Norwegian, and endeavored beforehand to master a few important phrases.

At the same time, Mr. Horner was occupied in laying out a plan for passing the month of July in Holland. The business which took him there was assuming greater importance, and from Mr. Agry, his partner in New York, now came letters of introduction to people in Amsterdam, and suggestions of steps to be taken.

The early history of Norway is enveloped in darkness, and rests on traditions dating from the eleventh and twelfth centuries. The Aborigines are descendants of a branch of the great Gothic stock. The early settlers formed, for a long period, numerous small communities, which waged continual war upon each other, until Harald Haarfager,

BERLIN: STATUE OF FREDERICK THE GREAT.

in 872, completed the conquest of them all. From this time, down to the middle of the thirteenth century, is comprised the heroic period of Norwegian history, replete with tales of grand warlike exploits, and great riches brought home by vikings.

Danes and Norwegians alike were called Northmen; the whole seaboard of Europe was visited by vikings, and they even penetrated to America; and many wise people think as far as New England.

The city of Trondhjem was founded A. D. 997, by King Olaf Trygvason. The adventures of this prince are the most romantic of all the sovereigns of Norway. Born a prince, his mother only saved his life from the usurper of his rights by quitting the country; they were taken by pirates, separated, and sold as slaves; at an early age he was discovered and redeemed by a relative, became a distinguished sea-king, married an Irish princess, embraced Christianity, and ultimately fought his way to the throne of Norway in 991. He then became a zealous missionary, propagating the faith by the sword. Death or Christianity was the only alternative he allowed his subjects. In the year 1008, he went over to England to the assistance of Ethelred the Unready, against the Danes, who, however, put Ethelred to flight, and took the English throne: and in 1028, Canute the Great landed in Norway. He was at that time the most powerful monarch in Europe, and called himself king of England, Denmark, Sweden and Norway. Upon his death, his son was driven from the throne, and the native line was resumed. These early kings were crowned at Bergen.

BERGEN.

Harold III. one of the greatest warriors of his age, invaded England, and was there slain in battle, fighting against Harold II. of England, who three weeks afterwards fell at Hastings, October 14th, 1066; thus ending the Saxon period in England.

A Norwegian king, Hagen VI., married a daughter of Denmark, and when, in 1380, the crown descended to his infant son, the two countries were united under the sceptre, and so remained down to 1814. The daughter of Hagen was a famous queen Margaret, known as the Semiramis of the North. She conquered Sweden, and united that country to her dominions; but her successors had not the ability to keep all the countries together. In 1523, Gustavus Vasa established the independence of that country, and shortly afterwards Norway was deprived of her parliament and reduced to a mere province of Denmark.

In 1536, the reformation was introduced, and gradually and peacefully established, and for three hundred years, under the rule of Denmark, the Norwegians took a considerable part in the literary and scientific life of Scandinavia, Copenhagen and its university being the intellectual centre.

In 1813, the allied powers arranged an odd plan of dividing these countries. Napoleon had signed away to Russia the Swedish province of Finland, which did not belong to him; Russia now indemnified Sweden by a present of Norway, to which she had no title, and England offered to Denmark an equivalent in lower Saxony, which was then in the possession of France. The Norwegians did not like their share in this bargaining. They were justly indignant at being thus transferred from Denmark to Sweden, without their consent, and determined to resist it and declare their independence. But resistance was useless. After several months, Christian VIII. abdicated the throne of Norway, and the king of Sweden was elected in his place November 4, 1814; but the most favorable terms were offered the Norwegians, and the first article of the constitution declares that "Norway shall be a free State, independent, indivisible, inalienable, united to Sweden under the same king." The present sovereign, Oscar II., and his queen, Sophia of Nassau, were crowned king and queen of Norway at the cathedral of Trondhjem, on the 18th July, 1873.

ANTWERP CATHEDRAL.

In Berlin, Bessie and all the rest of them failed not to see the emperor to their heart's content, once at the opera, where he sat in the royal box surrounded by his handsome family, benignly listening to the music, and again driving in the Thier-Garten. They admired his stalwart figure, and handsome genial countenance; but Bessie would not allow that he was anything more than a machine-made emperor, not at all to be compared with Barbarossa and Charlemagne. Wiser heads in the party were ready to give him the high place he deserves in the history of the century.

The Norwegians were to leave first, Mr. Horner wishing to see

TRONDHJEM CATHEDRAL.

them off, after which he, with Mrs. Horner and Philip, were to start direct for Cologne, and make no stop until they should reach Antwerp. This they successfully achieved, and their first letter, which was received by the others at Copenhagen, was dated within hearing of the chimes of the beautiful Gothic cathedral of that place.

www.ingramcontent.com/pod-product-compliance
Lightning Source LLC
Chambersburg PA
CBHW021809230426
43669CB00008B/690